A SKULL IN CONNEMARA

BY MARTIN McDONAGH

★

★

DRAMATISTS
PLAY SERVICE
INC.

SPECIAL NOTE

Anyone receiving permission to produce A SKULL IN CONNEMARA is required to give credit to the Author as sole and exclusive Author of the Play on the title page of all programs distributed in connection with performances of the Play and in all instances in which the title of the Play appears for purposes of advertising, publicizing or otherwise exploiting the Play and/or a production thereof. The name of the Author must appear on a separate line, in which no other name appears, immediately beneath the title and in size of type equal to 50% of the size of the largest, most prominent letter used for the title of the Play. No person, firm or entity may receive credit larger or more prominent than that accorded the Author. The following acknowledgment must appear on the title page in all programs distributed in connection with performances of the Play:

A SKULL IN CONNEMARA was first presented as
a Druid Theatre Company and Royal Court Theatre co-production
in Galway, Ireland and then in London in the summer of 1997.

SPECIAL NOTE ON SONGS AND RECORDINGS

For performances of copyrighted songs, arrangements or recordings mentioned in this Play, the permission of the copyright owner(s) must be obtained. Other songs, arrangements or recordings may be substituted provided permission from the copyright owner(s) of such songs, arrangements or recordings is obtained; or songs, arrangements or recordings in the public domain may be substituted.

2

A SKULL IN CONNEMARA was first produced by Druid Theatre Company (Garry Hynes, Artistic Director) and the Royal Court, at the Town Hall Theatre, in Galway, Ireland, on June 3, 1997, and then at the Royal Court Theatre Downstairs, in London, England, on July 17, 1997. It was directed by Garry Hynes; the set design was by Francis O'Connor; the lighting design was by Ben Ormerod; the sound design was by Bell Helicopter; the music was by Paddy Cunneen; and the production managers were Ed Wilson (RCT) and Maurice Power (Druid). The cast was as follows:

MICK DOWD. . . . . Mick Lally
MARY RAFFERTY. . . . . Anna Manahan
MAIRTIN HANLON . . . . David Wilmot
TOM HANLON . . . . Brían F. O'Byrne

CHARACTERS

MICK DOWD — fifties.
MARYJOHNNY RAFFERTY — seventies.
MAIRTIN HANLON — late teens/early twenties.
THOMAS HANLON — thirties.

SETTING

Rural Galway.

A SKULL IN CONNEMARA

SCENE ONE

The fairly spartan main room of a cottage in rural Galway. Front door stage left, a table with two chairs and a cupboard towards the right, and a lit fireplace in the centre of the back wall with an armchair on each side of it. A crucifix hangs on the back wall and an array of old farm tools, sickles, scythes and picks etc., hang just below it. At the start of the play, Mick Dowd, a man in his fifties whose cottage it is, is sitting in the left armchair as Mary Rafferty, a heavy-set, white-haired neighbour in her seventies, knocks and is let in through the front door.

MARY.   Mick.
MICK.   Maryjohnny.
MARY.   Cold.
MICK.   I suppose it's cold.
MARY.   Cold, aye. It's turning.
MICK.   Is it turning?
MARY.   It's turning now, Mick. The summer is going.
MICK.   It isn't going yet, or is it now?
MARY.   The summer is going, Mick.
MICK.   What month are we now?
MARY.   Are we September?
MICK.   *(Thinks.)* We are, d'you know?
MARY.   The summer is going.
MICK.   What summer we had.

MARY.   What summer we had. We had no summer.

MICK.   Sit down for yourself, there, Mary.

MARY.   *(Sitting.)* Rain, rain, rain, rain, rain we had. And now the cold. And now the dark closing in. The leaves'll be turning in a couple of weeks and that'll be the end of it.

MICK.   I didn't even know it *was* September, and I'll admit it.

MARY.   Did you not now, Mick? What month did you think it was?

MICK.   August or something I thought it was.

MARY.   August? *(Laughs.)* August is gone.

MICK.   I know it is, now.

MARY.   August went.

MICK.   I know it did.

MARY.   Last month August was.

MICK.   *(Slightly irritated.)* I know it was now, Mary. You don't have to keep saying.

MARY.   *(Pause.)* Didn't the boys and girls go back to school, and stopped parading up and down the street like....

MICK.   Ah sure they did. And don't I usually notice that one, and say to meself. 'The boys and girls have gone back to school. The summer is surely over now.'

MARY.   Like a pack o'whores.

MICK.   *(Pause.)* Who's like a pack o'whores?

MARY.   Them schoolies parading up and down.

MICK.   I wouldn't say a pack o'whores, now.

MARY.   Kissing.

MICK.   What harm?

MARY.   Cursing.

MICK.   Mary, you're too old-fashioned, so you are. Who doesn't curse nowadays?

MARY.   I don't.

MICK.   'You don't.'

MARY.   *(Pause.)* Eamonn Andrews didn't.

MICK.   Well we can't all be as good as you or Eamonn Andrews. And I'll bet Eamonn Andrews would've cursed too were he to've fell, or sat on a nail.

MARY.   He would not.

MICK.   It's only on television you ever saw. When he got home he probably cursed a-plenty. He probably did nothing but curse.

MARY. Oh, a lie now....

MICK. When he got home now, I'm saying.

MARY. I'll tell you someone else who doesn't curse. *(Pointing to the crucifix.)* That man doesn't curse.

MICK. Well we can't all be as good as Our Lord. Let alone Eamonn Andrews. Now those youngsters are only out for a bit of fun during their holidays, and not meaning no harm to anybody.

MARY. No harm to anybody, is it, Mick? And the three I caught weeing in the churchyard and when I told them I'd tell Father Cafferty, what did they call me? A fat oul biddy!

MICK. I know they did, Mary, and they shouldn't't've....

MARY. I know well they shouldn't't've!

MICK. That was twenty-seven years ago for God's sake, Mary.

MARY. Twenty-seven years ago or not!

MICK. You should let bygones be bygones.

MARY. Bygones, is it? No, I will not let bygones be bygones. I'll tell you when I'll let bygones be bygones. When I see them burned in Hell I'll let bygones be bygones, and not before!

MICK. Hell is too harsh a price just for weeing. Sure they were only five, God bless them.

MARY. On consecrated ground, Mick.

MICK. On consecrated ground or not. They may have been bursting. And what's consecrated ground anyways but any old ground with a dab of holy water pegged on it?

MARY. Well, you would be the man, Mick Dowd, I'd expect would argue that, the filthy occupation you take on every autumntime....

MICK. *(Interrupting.)* There's no need for that.

MARY. Is there no need for that, now? *(Mick gets up, pours out two glasses of poteen, gives one to Mary and sits down with the other.)*

MICK. Doesn't the County pay for the job to be done if it's such a filthy occupation? Doesn't the priest half the time stand over me and chat to me and bring me cups of tea? Eh?

MARY. *(Pause.)* I suppose he does. *(Sips her poteen.)* Not that I'd give a bent ha'-penny for that young skitter.

MICK. What young skitter?

MARY. Father Welsh, Walsh, Welsh.

MICK.   Nothing the matter with Father Welsh.

MARY.   Nothing the matter at all, except I don't too much like going to confession with a gasur aged two!

MICK.   What the Hell sins do you have to confess to him every week anyways?

MARY.   What sins do *you* confess would be more in your line.

MICK.   *(Playfully.)* What would it be, now? It wouldn't be impure thoughts? Ah no. It must be 'Thou shalt not steal' so.

MARY.   How, 'Thou shalt not steal'?

MICK.   Oh, cadging off the Yanks a pound of throw the maps the Tourist Board asked you to give them for free. Telling them your Liam's place was where *The Quiet Man* was filmed, when wasn't it a hundred miles away in Ma'am Cross or somewhere?

MARY.   A hundred miles is it? Ma'am Cross has moved so, because eight miles it was the last time I looked.

MICK.   John Wayne photos, two pound a pop. Maureen O'Hara drank out of this mug, a fiver. Boy, I'll tell you, anh? Them eejit Yanks.

MARY.   If the eejit Yanks want to contribute a couple of bob to an oul lady's retirement, I'll not be standing in their way, sure.

MICK.   So if it's not cadging off them thicks you confess it must be playing the ten books the bingo, so.

MARY.   *(Smiling.)* I don't play ten books the bingo.

MICK.   Oh, the County could round up a hundred witnesses would tell you the differ, 'cos twenty year it's been going on now.

MARY.   Maybe now and then I do forget how many books I've picked up....

MICK.   Forget, is it?

MARY.   *(Slightly hurt.)* It's forget, Mick. I do mean to pick up the four, and then two books get stuck together, and before I know where I am I'm sitting down and how many books do I have....

MICK.   Mary Rafferty, you have played ten books in that church hall for every week since de Valera was twelve, and it's ten books if they're lucky, because doesn't it rise to fifteen when the Christmas jackpot draws on, and isn't it twenty-two books at once your Guinness World's record is, and wouldn't it be higher still if it wasn't eighteen times you won that night and you thought they might begin to get suspicious? *(Mary stares at him angrily.)*

8

MARY. Well on the subject of confession, now, Mick Dowd, how long is it since *you've* seen the priest? Seven and a half years, is it, Mick?

MICK. Eh?

MARY. Seven and a half....

MICK. *(Angrily.)* That's enough of that, now, Mary.

MARY. Wasn't it your Oona used to drag you there of a week...?

MICK. *(Angrily, standing.)* That's enough of that now, I said! Or else be off with you! *(He idles a little, pouring himself another drink.)*

MARY. He calls too slow anyways.

MICK. Who calls to slow?

MARY. That skitter at St. Patrick's the bingo.

MICK. Oh, calls the bingo.

MARY. Walsh, Welsh. *(Pause.)* You need ten books to make it worthwhile, else you'd be hanging about, so. It isn't to win I have ten books.

MICK. It's the game of it.

MARY. It's the game of it, Mick, is right.

MICK. Nobody begrudges you anyways.

MARY. Because I'm oul.

MICK. Nobody begrudges you still. *(A knock at the front door, which pushes open immediately, Mairtin enters in a Man. Utd away shirt, blowing bubbles now and then.)*

MAIRTIN. How is all?

MARY. How are you, Mairtin?

MICK. How are you, Mairtin? And close the door.

MAIRTIN. I'll close the door *(Does so.)* or was it a barn with a wide open door you were born in, me mam says. She says, was it a barn with a wide open door you were born in, Mary beag, and I say 'You're the get would know, Mam.' *(Mary tuts.)* No, I say, you're the woman would know, Mam. I do. That's what I say, like. Because if anybody was to know where I was born, wouldn't it be her? *(Pause.)* The Regional Hospital I was born. In Galway.

MICK. We know where the Regional Hospital is.

MAIRTIN. Aye. *(To Mary.)* Wasn't it you was in there with your hip?

MARY. No.

MAIRTIN. It must've been somebody else so. Aye. Who was it? Somebody who fell down and was fat.

MICK. What is it you've come over about, Mairtin?

MAIRTIN. Father Welsh or Walsh sent me over. It was choir and I was disruptive. Is that poteen, Mick? You wouldn't spare a drop.

MICK. No I wouldn't.

MAIRTIN. Ah g'wan....

MARY. Why was you being disruptive in choir, Mairtin? You used to be a good little singer, God bless you.

MAIRTIN. Ah, a pack of oul shite they sing now. *(Mary tuts at his language.)* A pack of not very good songs they sing now, I mean. All wailing, and about fishes, and bears.

MICK. About fishes and bears, is it?

MAIRTIN. It is. That's what *I* said, like. They said no, the youngsters like these ones. What's the song they had us singing tonight? Something about if I was a bear I'd be happy enough, but I'm even more glad I'm human. Ah, a pile of oul wank it is. It's only really the Christmas carols I do like.

MICK. And in September you don't get too much call for them.

MAIRTIN. Is right, you don't. But I think they should have them all year, instead of the skitter they do, because they do make you very Christmassy, like.

MARY. How is mam and dad, Mairtin, I haven't seen them a few days?

MAIRTIN. Oh, grand indeed, now. Or anyway me mam's grand and me dad's as grand as a bastard of a get like him can be....

MARY. Mairtin. Your own father now.

MAIRTIN. My own father is right. And if he took his belt off to you for no reason at all eight times a week, it wouldn't be so quick you'd be saying 'Your own father now.' I'll tell you that.

MICK. And you don't do anything to deserve it, I suppose? Ah no.

MAIRTIN. Not a thing.

MICK. Not a thing, oh aye. Not even the guards' tyres got

slashed outside the disco in Carraroe, your pal Ray Dooley got nabbed for, someone else ran away.

MAIRTIN. Wasn't me now, Mick.

MICK. Oh no. Of course.

MAIRTIN. I have a bad leg anyways, and what were the guards doing in the disco that time of night anyway is what I'd like to know.

MICK. Routing out the yobbos who started the bottle fight that the two wee girls got taken the night to hospital from.

MAIRTIN. Well you'd think they'd have something better to do with their time.

MICK. Uh-huh. What was Welsh's message, Mairtin?

MAIRTIN. And maybe them two girls deserved a bottling anyways. You don't know the full facts.

MARY. Why would poor girls deserve a bottling, sure?

MAIRTIN. Every why. Maybe the piss out of a fella's trainers they took, when all he did was ask them for a danceen, and polite. And then called their bastard brother over to come the hard. Stitches aren't good enough for them sorts of bitches, and well they know. As ugly as them two started out, sure stitches'd be nothing but an improvement, oh aye. *(Pause.)* But as I say, I wasn't there, now, I had a bag leg.

MICK. Are you going to make me ask me question again, Mairtin?

MAIRTIN. What question?

MICK. What was Welsh's fecking message, for Christ's sake?!

MAIRTIN. *(Pause.)* Shouting is it, Mick? You're to make a start on this year's exhuming business this coming week. The grave-yard shenanigans. *(Mary looks across at Mick with stern resentment. Mick avoids her gaze somewhat guiltily.)*

MICK. This coming week? That's early. In the year, I mean. Although with them burying poor Mag Folan last month there I suppose has hurried things along a little.

MAIRTIN. I don't know if it's hurried things along a little and I don't care if it's hurried things along a little. I'm to help you anyways and twenty quid the week oul Walsh, oul Welsh is to be giving me.

11

MICK.   You're to help me?

MAIRTIN.   Oul Welsh said. Aye. Twenty quid the week. How much do you get the week, Mick?

MICK.   I get enough the week, and what matter is it to you?

MAIRTIN.   No matter at all, now. Only wondering, I was.

MICK.   Well don't be wondering.

MAIRTIN.   Sure, you're the experienced man, anyways. If it's a hundred or if it's more than a hundred, you deserve it, for you're the experienced man. *(Pause.)* Is it more than a hundred, Mick, now?

MICK.   This ladeen.

MAIRTIN.   Sure I'm only asking, sure.

MICK.   Well that's what you do best is ask eejit questions.

MAIRTIN.   Oh, eejit questions, is it?

MICK.   It is.

MAIRTIN.   Ah ... ah ... hmm.

MARY.   It's more than you, Mairtin, has questions that that man will not answer.

MICK.   Oh, now you're starting with your oul woman bull.

MAIRTIN.   What kind of questions, Mary beag?

MARY.   Questions about where did he put our Padraig when he dug him up is the kind of question, and where did he put our Bridgit when he dug her up is the kind of question, and where did he put my poor ma and da when he dug them up is the biggest question!

MAIRTIN.   Where *did* you put all Mary's relations, Mick, then, now? The oul bones and the whatnot.

MARY.   He won't let on.

MICK.   Will I not let on?

MARY.   Let on so.

MAIRTIN.   Aye, let on so.

MICK.   Oh, now you're chipping in.

MAIRTIN.   I *am* chipping in. What did you do with them?

MICK.   What did I do with them, is it?

MAIRTIN.   It is. For the hundredth fecking time it is.

MICK.   Oh, for the hundredth fecking time, is it? I'll tell you what I did with them. I hit them with a hammer until they were dust and I pegged them be the bucketload into the slurry. *(Mary is aghast. Mairtin bursts out laughing loudly.)*

MAIRTIN.   *(Laughing.)* Is that true, now?

MICK.   Oh, maybe it's true now, and maybe it isn't at all.

MAIRTIN.   You hit them with a hammer and you pegged them in the slurry? Can I do that, now, Mick?

MICK.   No, you can't do that.

MAIRTIN.   Ah, you don't hammer no corpses at all. Probably seal them up and put them somewhere is all you do. Put them in the lake or somewhere, when no beggar's about.

MICK.   Maybe it's in the lake I put them, aye. This is the expert. *(Mary has been keeping Mick in a stern, fixed stare all the while.)*

MARY.   Mick Dowd!

MICK.   Maryjohnny!

MARY.   I am going to ask you one question! And I want the truth!

MICK.   Ask away for yourself!

MARY.   Is that right what you said that you hammer the bones to nothing and you throw them in the slurry?

MICK.   What I do with the bones, both the priest and the guards have swore me to secrecy and bound by them I am....

MAIRTIN.   Oh ho.

MARY.   *(Standing.)* Michael Dowd, if you do not answer, bound or not bound, I shall leave this devil-taken house and never darken its...!

MICK.   Bound I am by the priest and the guards....

MARY.   Michael Dowd, if you do not answer....

MICK.   I neither hammer the bones nor throw them in the slurry, Mary. Sure what do you take me for?

MAIRTIN.   I knew well, sure....

MARY.   So what is it you do with them so, if it isn't hammer?

MICK.   *(Pause.)* I seal them in a bag and let them sink to the bottom of the lake and a string of prayers I say over them as I'm doing so.

MAIRTIN.   I told you, now, it was the fecking lake, or the lake rather. Didn't I tell you now that that's what it was, that he sealed them in a bag and he pegged them in the lake?

MICK.   I didn't say I pegged them. I said I gently *eased* them.

13

MAIRTIN. Oh, aye, you eased them in there, like. And said a couple of prayers over them, aye.

MICK. And said a couple of prayers over them.

MAIRTIN. To make it official, like.

MARY. Is that the truth, Mick Dowd?

MICK. That's the truth, Mary beag.

MARY. I shall sit and finish that sup with you, so.

MICK. Good on you, Mary. *(Mary sits back down. Mick refills her glass.)*

MAIRTIN. *(Eyeing the poteen.)* After seven years, sure, it's only a poor straggle of two or three bones they are anyway, I'm sure, and nothing to hammer at all.

MICK. The expert on the matter now we're listening to.

MAIRTIN. It's nothing to do with expert. Pure oul common sense is all it has to do with.

MICK. Now you're explaining it to me.

MAIRTIN. There's been a cow in our field dead four or five years....

MICK. I know there has. And that's the best cow you have.

MAIRTIN. No, no, now. Not the best cow we have. It wasn't even our cow at all. Didn't it just wander into our fields one day and fall over dead?

MICK. Aye. The smell knocked it.

MAIRTIN. And isn't it now just the ... 'The smell knocked it.' Feck you. The smell of this house? Eh? 'The smell knocked it'? I'll tell you boy, eh? *(Pause.)* What was it I was saying, now? You've made me forget....

MICK. 'Isn't it now just the' something....

MAIRTIN. Isn't it now just the skull and a couple of bones left on it, the cow, and no hide nor hair other than that? So wouldn't the body of a person be even less than that, it being rotting in the ground?

MICK. You have a point there. Except the body of a person your family wouldn't have been picking at for yere dinners the last five years.

MAIRTIN. Picking at it for our dinners, is it? We do have a sight better dinners in our house than you do in this fecking house anyways! I'll tell you that now! Poteen breakfasts and poteen suppers is all I even see consumed in this house!

MICK.   True enough for yourself.

MAIRTIN.   Eh? Insulting our mam's dinners, when all it was was explaining about the cow in our field and the bones was all I was doing. Explaining, so as to help you.

MICK.   You're right there, now, Mairtin, I wasn't thinking.

MAIRTIN.   Right? I know I'm right.

MICK.   And if I insulted you or your mam or your mam's dinners by casting aspersions you pick the meat off cows five years dead and can't tell the differ, then I take it all back and I apologise.

MAIRTIN.   *(Confused.)* Eh? Uh-huh? Well, okay. Good. *(Mick pours himself another drink.)* And just to show there's no hard feelings, the tiniest of sips, now, let me take a taste of, Mick. This much, even.

MICK.   That much, is it?

MAIRTIN.   That's all. To show there's no hard feelings, now.

MICK.   To show there's no hard feelings, aye. *(He pours a small amount of poteen out onto his fingers and tosses it at Mairtin as if it's holy water. It hits Mairtin in the eyes.)* Bless yourself, now, Mairtin. *(Mary laughs slightly. Mick sits back down. Mairtin rubs his eyes angrily.)*

MAIRTIN.   Got me in the eye, that did!

MICK.   Sure that's where I was aiming. I'll bet it stung too.

MAIRTIN.   It *did* sting too, you stinking fecker you. *(Mary tuts.)* Tut at me, you? Tut at him would be more in your line when he throws poteen in me eyes, near blinds me.

MARY.   You'll know now not again to be disruptive in choir, Mairtin beag.

MAIRTIN.   Choir?! What has fecking choir to do with anything?! He insults me mam's cooking, throws poteen in me eyes.

MICK.   Sure it was only a drop, sure. Would I be wasting good poteen on your eyes?

MAIRTIN.   *(To Mary.)* Has it gone red, Gran?

MARY.   A bit red, Mairtin....

MICK.   'Gone red'. Jeez, you always was a wussy oul pussy, Mairtin, and nothing but a wussy oul pussy.

MAIRTIN.   A wussy oul pussy, is it?

MICK.   It is.

MAIRTIN.   Well maybe I am at that, and maybe I know some-thing that you don't know too.

MICK.   What do you know? Skitter you know, Mairtin beag.

MAIRTIN.   Maybe I know which corner of the cemetery it is we're to be digging this week.

MICK.   What do I care which corner of the cemetery?

MAIRTIN.   Oh, maybe you don't, now. Only that it's the south side, by the gable. *(Mick nods, somewhat disturbed.)*

MICK.   Are they all more than seven years down, then, at the gable. They are, I suppose.

MAIRTIN.   They are. Seven years and more! *(To Mary.)* See? He doesn't like it when it starts to get closer to home. That's when he doesn't like it.

MARY.   What do you mean, 'closer to home'?

MAIRTIN.   Isn't it his missus buried down there by the gable? How closer to home can you get?

MARY.   Is Oona buried at the gable, Mick, now?

MICK.   She is.

MARY.   Oh, God love you....

MAIRTIN.   That'll be an interesting job anyways. It isn't many's the man gets paid for digging up the bones of his own dead wife.

MICK.   Oona left those bones a long time ago, and that's the only thing that they are now is bones.

MARY.   *(Quietly.)* You can't go digging up Oona, Mick. That's not right. Leave Oona to somebody else, now.

MICK.   To who? To him? He'd probably crack her head in two, so he would.

MAIRTIN.   Oh, crack her head in two, is it?

MICK.   It is.

MAIRTIN.   I heard that's already been done.

MICK.   *(Pause. Standing, advancing.)* What did you hear?

MAIRTIN.   Just a thing or two, now, and don't you be fecking advancing on me, because saying nothing I was, only some people say things and I pay no mind at all until some other people start shouting the odds and calling me names and peg-ging poteen in my eyes....

MICK.   What names did I call you?

MARY.   *(Pause. Quietly.)* A wussy oul pussy....

16

MAIRTIN. A wussy oul pussy you called me. And if people start doing that then I'll have to be pegging something back at them, and it isn't a smatter of poteen it'll be, it'll be aspersions. And if the aspersions are true or not I don't know, and I don't care. I only threw them out because it was you who started the whole shebang in the first place.

MICK. What *are* the aspersions anyways?

MAIRTIN. Just general ones.

MICK. The only aspersions that could be cast are the ones I've already admitted to, and the ones I've already served me time over. That I had had a drink taken, and a good drink, and that she had no seat-belt on her, and that was the end of it. No other aspersions could there be.

MAIRTIN. Well, sure, that was the aspersion I was saying anyways, the drink-driving aspersion. What aspersion did you think I was saying?

MICK. *(Pause.)* That was the aspersion you was saying?

MAIRTIN. Aye. *(Pause.)* What was....

MICK. Well even that aspersion is seven years past, yet straight to me face you go casting your fecking....

MAIRTIN. Well isn't that better than the most of them round here? Will smile at you 'til you're a mile away before they start talking behind your back. One thing about me, anyways, I'm honest.

MICK. *(To Mary.)* Do people be talking behind my back?

MARY. They do not. He's a wee get with nothing but cheek.

MAIRTIN. A wee get is it? And they don't be talking behind his back? Uh-huh. It must be some other fella who drove his wife into a wall, so, they must be talking about. I must be mistaken. I often am.

MICK. *(Quietly.)* Leave this house, Mairtin Hanlon.

MAIRTIN. I *will* leave this house, the welcome I got here, after coming all this way with the message from oul Welsh, Walsh, Welsh. Not only no welcome but a spray of poteen that almost took me eyes out as a thank you, not to mention the names called, and the insulted mam's dinners. Uh-huh. *(Exits. Reenters)* Um ... will they have a spade at the church I can use, Mick, for I have no spade?

17

MARY. Your father has a rake of spades, sure.

MAIRTIN. My father has no rake of spades. He as a rake of rakes. He has no spade. The only spade he has are the handles of two spades, and nothing but the handles, which you couldn't call a spade at all. Rakes he has a stack of, and I don't know why, because there is no call for them. There is always more call for a spade than a rake. In my opinion.

MICK. They'll have a spade at the church.

MAIRTIN. Will they have a spade at the church? Except they'll need two spades. One for the both of us....

MICK. They'll have two spades.

MAIRTIN. Are you positive, now? I don't want to be walking all that way....

MICK. Mairtin, will you ever feck off home for yourself?!

MAIRTIN. Feck off home, is it? I'll feck off home, all right. I don't have to be asked twice.

MICK. No, fecking five times you have to be asked!

MAIRTIN. *(Exiting.)* Uh-huh, I don't have to be asked twice.

MARY. *(Pause.)* The tongue on that one. *(Pause. They drink their poteen a while, staring into the fire.)*

MICK. Is it true, Mary?

MARY. Is what true, Mick?

MICK. The talking behind my back.

MARY. There is no talking behind your back. He's a wee eejit, or if not an eejit then a blackguard, and we both know the truth of that.

MICK. Aye.

MARY. Sure the time he put the werewolf comic in with Mrs. Dunphy, and hadn't they almost nailed the lid on her before we noticed?

MICK. Aye.

MARY. If that had gone ahead, just think. *(Pause.)* The boy's a wee blackguard and nothing else, and even though he's me own grandson I'll admit it, he's a rotten blackguard with nothing but cheek, so don't you even be thinking about it.

MICK. Aye. *(Pause.)* Aye, I suppose you're right.

MARY. I *am* right, sure.

MICK. Aye.

MARY. Right? There's no question, right.

MICK. There's not, I suppose. No. *(Pause.)* No. *(Pause.)* And there's been no other aspersions cast with my name on them, other than those....

MARY. There's been no other aspersions, Mick. *(Pause.)* None at all, sure. *(Pause.)* Sure we all know the type of man you are, Mick Dowd. *(Mick looks across at her.)*

MICK. Aye.... Is right. *(Mary smiles at him slightly. They both stare at the fire again. Curtain.)*

SCENE TWO

A rocky cemetery at night, lit somewhat eerily by a few lamps dotted about. Two graves with gravestones atop a slight incline in the centre. At the start of the scene, the grave on the right is in the process of being dug up by Mick, standing down inside it to waist height, shoveling the dirt out. Mairtin lays his shovel down, sits against the right hand gravestone behind him, and lights a cigarette.

MAIRTIN. I'm taking a cigarette break.

MICK. A break from what, sure? You've done no work.

MAIRTIN. I've done my biteen.

MICK. A bit of shite you've done.

MAIRTIN. I have a blister too, and I didn't even mention it.

MICK. You've mentioned it now.

MAIRTIN. For fear I'd be accused of complaining. *(Pause. Looking at the next-door grave.)* When will we be starting on your missus's patch anyways? Going around in circles to avoid it we seem to be.

MICK. We go in order. We don't skip two ahead.

MAIRTIN. Skip? That's all we've been doing is skipping, if you're asking my opinion. *(Pause.)* I'll make a start on your missus's grave.

19

MICK. Will you, now?

MAIRTIN. I may. *(Mairtin takes his shovel and idles past Mick to Oona's grave. Mick stops work and looks at him threateningly. Mairtin taps the soil with his foot, then raises his shovel as if about to start digging.)*

MICK. One grain of that soil you touch, Mairtin Hanlon, it is *in* that grave you will be, not on it. *(Mairtin smiles, lays his shovel aside, and leans against the gravestone behind him.)*

MAIRTIN. Is it murder you're threatening now, Mick, and in earshot of your missus too?

MICK. It isn't murder, because self-defence it would be, as protection from your wittering on like a fecking oul hen. I would be doing the community a service.

MAIRTIN. The community a service? I heard you already did the community a service.

MICK. What service?

MAIRTIN. The community service you did, when they let you out of jail early.

MICK. Now you're starting again. *(Mick returns to his digging.)*

MAIRTIN. I'm just saying, like.

MICK. Now you're trying to come the clever.

MAIRTIN. Well, as I say to Sheila Fahey, it isn't too hard I have to try to come the clever, because I *am* clever.

MICK. Clever, is it? And is it ten times you've failed the Leaving Certificate now, or is it eleven times?

MAIRTIN. It's one time.

MICK. Oh, is it one time, now?

MAIRTIN. The other time it coincided with me wrongful expulsion.

MICK. Your wrongful expulsion? Uh-huh. The cat you cooked alive in biology?

MAIRTIN. It wasn't me at all now, Mick, and they knew full well it wasn't me, and didn't they have to reinstate me on the spot when Blind Billy Pender came out and confessed, with not a word of apology from them.

MICK. Poor backward Blind Billy Pender, aye, whom you didn't influence in his confession at all.

MAIRTIN. And it was a hamster anyways, if you would like to get your facts right.

MICK. I don't need help from the likes of you to get me facts right.

MAIRTIN. Oh aye.

MICK. I'll tell you that anyways.

MAIRTIN. *(Pause.)* Let's get a start on your missus's grave, Mick.

MICK. *(Pause.)* We'll get a start when we've finished this one. And when the guard arrives.

MAIRTIN. When the guard arrives? Oh. Is there a law, so, you can't dig up your wife unless you have the polis there?

MICK. Something of the like. Or, anyways, the guard had a word, said I'd best make sure he was there before we made a start. To save tongues wagging anyways.

MAIRTIN. What would tongues be wagging for?

MICK. I don't know. Just for the sake of it. *(Sound of Mick's shovel hitting the rotten wood at the bottom of the grave.)*

MAIRTIN. Are you through to him?

MICK. Pass me the sack down. *(Mairtin jumps up from where he is and looks down into the grave. Sound of Mick jimmying rotten wood apart with his shovel. He picks the bits of wood up and throws them out of the grave. Mairtin moves around a little to get a better view of the corpse.)*

MAIRTIN. Ay yi yi, look at that one. Who is he? *(Glances behind.)* Daniel Faragher. Never heard of him.

MICK. I knew him to say hello to.

MAIRTIN. Would you recognise him? *(Mick looks at Mairtin as if he's stupid.)* Not from his bare skull, no, of course. Although he still has a lock of hair there, now. He looks like a big dolly.

MICK. A what?

MAIRTIN. A big dolly. Like girls do play with.

MICK. The girls won't be playing with this dolly.

MAIRTIN. I know that, sure. I'm only saying. How old would he be, then?

MICK. He would be....

MAIRTIN. No, let me guess, now.

MICK.   Guess ahead.

MAIRTIN.   A pound if I guess right.

MICK.   And a pound to me if you guess wrong.

MAIRTIN.   Okay. *(Glances at headstone and calculates.)* He was, I'd say ... about sixty-seven now.

MICK.   Wrong. *Seventy*-seven he was. You owe me a pound. *(Mairtin looks back at the headstone again, recalculates on his fingers, and realises his mistake.)*

MAIRTIN.   Ah feck.

MICK.   And pass me the sack, for the fiftieth time. *(Mairtin goes off mumbling behind the headstone.)*

MAIRTIN.   I'll pass you the fecking sack.... *(And returns with a large, dirty black cloth sack half-full of the bones and skulls of two corpses. Mairtin passes it to Mick.)* Pass your skull to me, Mick. Just to compare, now. *(Mick tosses Mairtin the skull with the lock of hair on it, then starts placing the bones from the grave into the sack, keeping a quiet eye on Mairtin all the while as he idles around with the skulls, placing them against his chest as if they're breasts at one point, kissing them together at another.)* Sure skulls are great oul things. It's hard to believe you have one of these on the inside of your head.

MICK.   It's hard to believe *you* have one of them anyways, and the brain to go with it.

MAIRTIN.   I have no brain, is it? I have a brain too, and a big brain.

MICK.   Kissing skulls together. Like an oul schoolgirl.

MAIRTIN.   *(Pause.)* When do oul schoolgirls kiss skulls together, sure?

MICK.   *(Pause.)* I'm just saying, like.

MAIRTIN.   Oul schoolgirls can't get ahold of skulls at all. *(He pokes a finger in the skulls' eye sockets.)* You can stick your fingers right in their eyes.

MICK.   *(Pause. Confused.)* Oul schoolgirls' eyes, now?

MAIRTIN.   Skulls' eyes, now! Why would you be sticking your fingers in schoolgirls' eyes?

MICK.   I don't know, now. *(Mairtin hands the skulls back to Mick who places them in the sack, then quietly crouches down and looks into the grave.)*

MAIRTIN.   Hey, Mick!

MICK. What?

MAIRTIN. Where does your thing go?

MICK. Eh?

MAIRTIN. Where does your thing go? When you die, I mean. None of them have had their things at all. And I've looked.

MICK. I know well you've looked. And the women's too! I think that's why you came on this job, to have a good look. You don't see many livings ones.

MAIRTIN. I see my share.

MICK. Of willies, now, Mairtin?

MAIRTIN. Of the other, and you know well!

MICK. Do you really not know where they go? Have you never been told?

MAIRTIN. No.

MICK. They don't tell you in religious studies?

MAIRTIN. No. I do skip a lot of religious studies. It's just a lot of stuff about Jesus.

MICK. That's the reason you don't know, so. Isn't it illegal in the Catholic faith to bury a body the willy still attached? Isn't it a sin in the eyes of the Lord?

MAIRTIN. *(Incredulous.)* No....

MICK. Don't they snip them off in the coffin and sell them to tinkers as dog food.

MAIRTIN. *(Horrified.)* They do not!

MICK. And during the famine, didn't the tinkers stop feeding them to their dogs at all and start sampling the merchandise themselves?

MAIRTIN. They did not, now, Mick....

MICK. You would see them riding along with them, munching ahead.

MAIRTIN. No....

MICK. That's the trouble with young people today, is they don't know the first thing about Irish history. *(Mick smiles to himself. Mairtin, sickened, sees this and begins to doubt.)*

MAIRTIN. That isn't true.

MICK. As true as I'm standing here.

MAIRTIN. I'll go up and ask oul Walsh, Welsh, at the church so. He'd be the man to know.

MICK. Go ahead, so.

MAIRTIN. Eh?

MICK. Go on ahead and ask for yourself.

MAIRTIN. I *will* go on ahead and ask.

MICK. Go so.

MAIRTIN. *(Pause.)* And ask do they cut the willies off and give them to tinkers?

MICK. Aye.

MAIRTIN. *(Pause.)* I'll go so.

MICK. So go.

MAIRTIN. I'm going. I don't need you to tell me to be going. *(Mairtin slowly idles off stage, L. Mick smiles to himself when he's gone, then gets out of the grave he's in, having finished collecting its bones, lifts the sack out with him and puts it to one side. He idles over stage L. to his wife's grave and looks down at it a while, hands in pockets. Enter the guard, Thomas Hanlon, stage R., in full uniform, sucking on, at intervals throughout, a cigarette and an asthma inhaler.)*

THOMAS. You haven't started?

MICK. I haven't started.

THOMAS. What are you doing so?

MICK. I'm just looking at it.

THOMAS. Oh aye. No harm. I had some trouble out at the Riordan's Hall is why I'm late. Two women fighting and one man.

MICK. Was the two women fighting the man or who was fighting who?

THOMAS. The two women was fighting among themselves and getting on fine when this oul fella butted in saying 'It's not right women fighting, break it up', and didn't the two of them deck him and take it in turns treading on him?

MICK. Good enough for him. What business was it of his them fighting. I like a good fight between women.

THOMAS. The same as that, I like a good fight between women, although I couldn't say that while on duty, like. We arrested the lot of them anyways. The oul fella couldn't believe it. Went crying he did. Crying and wouldn't stop crying. And Johnny Doyle said 'I'll give you a batter too if you don't stop', but even then he wouldn't stop.

MICK. Did he give him a batter so?

THOMAS. Ah no, now. There's no call to batter oul fellas, even if they're crying.

MICK. There's not I suppose.

THOMAS. Ah no. Sure we'll be oul fellas too someday.

MICK. *(Pause.)* I'll get a start on this, so.

THOMAS. Go ahead for yourself, aye. *(Mick starts digging up his wife's grave. Thomas sits against the right-hand headstone and looks inside the black sack, grimacing a little.)* Awful morbid work this is, Mick.

MICK. It's work to be done.

THOMAS. Awful ghoulish though.

MICK. Work to be done it is. Isn't the space needed?

THOMAS. I'm certain there are other ways. Encouraging cremation is what the church should be. Not all this.

MICK. Who around here would go for cremation? No one.

THOMAS. It's got to be better than this every year.

MICK. Get onto them so. *(Pause.)* Don't you come across more morbid things than this in your work every day? People only minutes dead you come across, neverminding seven years.

THOMAS. When do I come across people only minutes dead?

MICK. Do you not? Oh. I thought the way you do talk about it, just like *Hill Street Blues* your job is. Bodies flying about everywhere.

THOMAS. I would *like* there to be bodies flying about everywhere, but there never is.

MICK. Go ahead up north so. You'll be well away. Hang about a bookies or somewhere.

THOMAS. Ah there's no detective work in that oul bullshit. Detective work I'm talking about. You know, like *Quincy*.

MICK. Oh, like *Quincy*. *(Pause.)* Have you never seen a dead body, so? A just dead body?

THOMAS. The only body I've ever seen was a fella in a block of flats the road to Shannon. The fattest bastard you've ever seen in your life. Tits like this. Sitting, no clothes, in his armchair. No clothes, now. Television still on. A heart attack, the doctor said. All well and good. He knows more than me. But I had meself a look in that fat man's fridge, now. A mighty fridge it was, six feet high. What was in there? A pot of jam and a lettuce. Eh? And nothing else. A pot of jam and a lettuce in the fridge of the fattest man you've ever seen in your life. Nothing suspicious in that? I pointed it out in my report to them, and they just laughed at me. And watching television stark naked too? Nothing suspicious in that?

MICK. *(Pause.)* What time of year was it?

THOMAS. What time of year? I don't know....

MICK. If it was the height of summer, and he wasn't expecting any visitors, it might very well explain the stark naked.

THOMAS. *(Pause.)* It might explain the stark naked, aye. It might not explain the complete absence of food in his six-foot fridge! Eh?

MICK. You have a point.

THOMAS. I have a point, aye. I know I have a point. The amount of food a fat fella eats? He won't get far on a lettuce and a pot of jam! Just laughed at me they did. *(Pause.)* Where's the young shite anyways?

MICK. Gone up to the church. I told him to ask the priest is it right the Church hands out the willies of the dead to passing tinker children to play with.

THOMAS. And he hasn't gone?

MICK. He has gone.

THOMAS. Oh he's as thick as five thick fellas, that fecker. What do they teach them in school now anyways?

MICK. I don't know what they teach them. Cooking cats they teach them.

THOMAS. Cooking cats, aye. No. A hamster it was.

MICK. It's the same difference. Sure.

THOMAS. Pardon me?

MICK. It's the same difference, I said.

THOMAS. It's not the same difference at all, sure. A cat is one thing. A hamster is another.

MICK. Is it worth the argue, now?

THOMAS. I'm just saying, like. *(Pause.)* A fact is a fact, like. It's the same in detective work. No matter how small a detail may appear to be, you can't go lumping it with a bunch of other details like it's all the same thing. So you can't go lumping cats and hamsters together either. Things like that are the difference between solving and not solving an entire case, sure.

MICK. Oh aye, aye, they are, I suppose. *(Mick returns to his digging.)*

THOMAS. They are. They certainly are. Oh aye. *(Pause.)* How far are you down?

MICK. I'm down a good way. Funny, this soil's easy digging.... *(Mairtin returns, angry, rubbing his cheek.)*

MAIRTIN. A back-fecking-hander the fecker gave me, you fecking bastard ya! *(Mick and Thomas laugh.)* What the feck are yous laughing for, you feckers you?

THOMAS. Stop your cursing now, Mairtin. Not in the grave-yard. Against God so it is.

MAIRTIN. Against God, is it?

THOMAS. It is.

MAIRTIN. Feck God so! And his mother too! *(Both Mick and Thomas stop to chastise Mairtin, Thomas standing.)*

MICK. Hey...!!

THOMAS. Now, Mairtin, I'm liable to give you a batter meself if you go on like that, and a better batter it will be than the one you got from that biteen of a priest.

MAIRTIN. Ah, go to blazes with you.

THOMAS. A bloody better batter it will be.

MAIRTIN. Of course. Aren't the polis the experts at battering gasurs anyway? Don't you get a bonus for it? *(Mick continues digging.)*

THOMAS. What gasurs do I ever batter?

MAIRTIN. Ray Dooley for a start-off, or if not you then your bastarding cohorts.

THOMAS. What about Ray Dooley?

MAIRTIN. Didn't he end up the County Hospital ten minutes after you arrested him?

THOMAS. He did, the pisshead, a broken toe. Kicking the cell door in and forgetting he had no shoes on him.

MAIRTIN. Aye, that's what *you* say. That's way *you* say.

THOMAS. *(Pause.)* Don't be cursing God in a graveyard, anyway, is what the crux of the matter is.

MAIRTIN. Aye, and don't be invading people's human rights

27

is what the other crux of the matter is. The guards are there to serve the people, not the other way round, if you'd like to know.

THOMAS.   You've been paying attention in Sociology class anyways, Mairtin.

MAIRTIN.   I have.

THOMAS.   That's a good thing. Is it still Miss Byrne with the mini-skirts teaches that?

MAIRTIN.   I'm not bandying around pleasantries with the likes of you!

MICK.   Get back to fecking work, so, and start filling that one in. *(Mairtin tuts and goes to the right-hand grave with his shovel. He starts tipping the dirt back into it.)*

MAIRTIN.   *(To Thomas.)* I see you say nothing to him when he says 'feck' in the graveyard. Is it only kids, so you go shouting the odds with?

THOMAS.   It is, aye. Only kids.

MAIRTIN.   I know well it is.

THOMAS.   I do like to specialise.

MAIRTIN.   I know you do. *(Pause. Mumbling.)* Specialise me black arsehole. *(As Mairtin continues shoveling dirt at the grave's edge, Thomas quietly walks up behind him and shoves him down into it. Mairtin yelps. Mick and Thomas laugh, kicking dirt down onto him. Mairtin quickly clambers up from the rotten coffin underfoot.)* You're a fecking fecker, Thomas. And you're nothing else.

THOMAS.   *(Laughing.)* Haven't I told you, now, about your language.

MAIRTIN.   I'm going the feck home.

THOMAS.   You're not going the feck home either. I've told Dad to give you a batter himself if you're home before daybreak. So there you are.

MAIRTIN.   You're always ganging up on me, the fecking two of ye.

THOMAS.   Ah, the babby's going crying now. Go on and help Mick, whiny, or I'll tell oul Welsh to be docking your wages on you.

MAIRTIN.   *(Pause.)* Do you need help with the digging there, Mick?

MICK. No. Go on ahead with your filling in that one. *(Mairtin does so. Thomas lights a cigarette.)*
THOMAS. *(Pause.)* Aren't you getting nervous there now, Mick? I'd be nervous, seeing me wife again after such a time.
MICK. What's to be nervous for?
MAIRTIN. Aye, what's to be nervous for?
THOMAS. Nothing at all, now.
MICK. Nothing at all is right.
THOMAS. Aye, now. Only I thought you might have some things on your mind might be making you nervous seeing your missus again.
MICK. What kind of things on me mind?
MAIRTIN. Aye, what kind of things on his mind?
THOMAS. I don't know, now, I have no idea at all. Just things on your mind, like.
MICK. I have no things on me mind.
THOMAS. Good-oh, I was just saying, like.
MICK. What things are you saying I have on me mind?
THOMAS. No things at all, sure. None at all. Just conversing we are.
MICK. Conversing me arse. Do you have something to say to me?
THOMAS. No, no, now....
MICK. Because if you do, go ahead and spit it out. Is it me drink-driving you're saying?
THOMAS. I was saying nothing, now, Mick.
MICK. Casting aspersions on me...?
THOMAS. I was casting no aspersions at all....
MICK. The family of eejits and blackguards you come from?
MAIRTIN. *(Pause.)* Who's an eejit and a blackguard? Is it me he's talking about, Thomas?
THOMAS. It is, aye.
MAIRTIN. *(Pause.)* How do you know it's me he's talking about? It could've been you or Dad or anybody he was talking about.
THOMAS. Who are you talking about, Mick?
MICK. Him.

THOMAS. *(To Mairtin.)* See?

MAIRTIN. Ya feck!

THOMAS. Now, Mick, you've insulted poor wee Mairtin there, you've insulted family, such as it is, so now I have to go and say something insulting back to you. That is the way that these things operate.

MICK. You're the one who started with the insults.

THOMAS. No, Mick, no. I have to take you up on that. You're the one who started with the insults. I was the one who started with the vague insinuations.

MICK. It's the self-same thing.

THOMAS. Pardon me?

MICK. It's the self-same thing, I said.

THOMAS. It's not the self-same thing at all, and if you knew anything about the law then you'd know it's not the self-same thing. So now I have to turn me vague insinuations into something more of an insult, so then we'll all be quits....

MAIRTIN. *(To Mick.)* Your ma was a queer and your da was a queer and how they came up with you is a mystery of the Universe! *(Both Mick and Thomas stare blankly at Mairtin for a few moments, who looks away, embarrassed. Pause.)*

THOMAS. No, what I was going to say was ... some insinuation along the lines of ... not that I'm making any accusations, mind ... but maybe your wife's head injuries all those years ago weren't especially conducive to only having been in a car crash at all, and maybe....

MICK. *(Angrily.)* All that came out at the time, Thomas Hanlon, and didn't the inquest shoot every word of it down!

THOMAS. Y'know, maybe she was already dead *before* you drove her into the wall, that kind of insinuation, like. But nothing harsher than that am I saying.

MICK. Take all of that back, Thomas Hanlon!

THOMAS. I'm only suggesting, now, like.

MICK. Take every word of it back, because if you make me get up out of this grave, now, polis or not....

THOMAS. You take eejit and blackguard back, so, and I'll be pleased to take it back.

MICK. You take your things back first.

THOMAS. No, now. You said your things first, so it's only fair you take them back first too.

MICK. There was no call for any of this.

THOMAS. I agree with you, like.

MICK. For any of these insults. *(Pause.)* I take eejit and black-guard back.

THOMAS. I take wife-butcherer back, so. *(Mairtin laughs loudly, half in surprise, half in pride, as Mick and Thomas stare at each other.)*

MAIRTIN. Is that all true?

MICK. A pure drink-driving it was, Thomas, and you know full well it was.

THOMAS. I *do* know full well it was, and I've taken me accusations back without reservation.

MAIRTIN. Is it true, Thomas?

THOMAS. Of course it's not true, Mairtin. Haven't I just said? I made up every word of it.

MAIRTIN. *(Confused.)* I thought you were saying it was true.

THOMAS. Not at all. A pure drink-driving is all it was, just like Mick says. *(Mick and Thomas stare at each other a few seconds more, then Mick returns to his digging.)*

MAIRTIN. Oh-h. I'm disappointed so.

THOMAS. Why are you disappointed, babby?

MAIRTIN. There you got me hoping I was working with a fella up and slaughtered his wife with an axe or something, when all it was was an oul cheap-ass drink-driving. Aren't they ten-a-penny? Wouldn't it be hard to find somebody round here who *hasn't* killed somebody drink-driving? Or if not a somebody then a heifer, or at least a dog. Didn't oul Marcus Rigby kill twins with his tractor, and him over seventy?

THOMAS. No, he did not.

MAIRTIN. Did he not? Who was it killed twins with his tractor so? It was someone.

THOMAS. No. That was just something I told you when you was twelve to mind you kept out of the road with your bicycle when you saw a tractor coming.

31

MAIRTIN. *(Pause.)* There was no twins at all?

THOMAS. If you had any sense you'd have known when did ever twins live around here?

MAIRTIN. Twins come over from America I was thinking, to see where *The Quiet Man* was filmed and got lost.

THOMAS. You was thinking wrong, so. I only said twins to get you thinking if a tractor killed two gasurs it'd be twice as likely a tractor'd kill you, there only being one of you.

MAIRTIN. *(Angrily.)* So all those years I drove me bicycle through hedgerows and banks of skitter and all on account of them poor mangled twins I had on me mind, and it was all for nothing?!

THOMAS. *(Laughing.)* It was, indeed.

MAIRTIN. You're a bastard of a bastard of a bastard of a feck, Thomas Hanlon.

THOMAS. You're still alive anyways, is the main thing. Do you know how many boys the age of eight died falling into slurry tanks the last year in Ireland alone?

MAIRTIN. I don't! And I don't fecking care!

THOMAS. Fourteen. Fourteen of the poor gasurs.

MAIRTIN. Good! And let them die!

THOMAS. And drowning in slurry, Mairtin beag, isn't the nicest way to go out of this world. I'll tell you that for yourself.

MAIRTIN. Feck drowning in slurry, and feck their mothers too...!

MICK. *(Interrupting.)* That's not true, now, is it, Thomas? The fourteen gasurs drowning in the slurry?

THOMAS. It *is* true, aye. *(Pause.)* Not altogether, mind....

MICK. No.

THOMAS. Not all in the one tank, now. Separately.

MICK. Separately. In different parts of the country, like, and at different times.

THOMAS. Aye. From the Central Office of Statistics this is. They have good statistics they do. More kids die in slurry tanks than die in combine harvesters. Only seven died in combine harvesters.

MICK. Of course. Because more people have slurry tanks than have combine harvesters.

THOMAS.   That's true enough.

MICK.   It's only rich people have combine harvesters. And their kids are less thick anyways.

THOMAS.   Is right.

MICK.   To go climbing in slurry you have to be thick.

THOMAS.   You do.

MAIRTIN.   *(Angrily.)* It wasn't climbing in slurry this conversation was at all! This conversation was the lie about the dead twins! *(As he speaks, Thomas pushes Mairtin over into the grave again and kicks dirt at him.)*

THOMAS.   Ah, shut your creeping bollocks about the dead twins, ya fecking oul shite-arse ya, and you're nothing else.

MAIRTIN.   Kick dirt at me, is it?! And ... and call me an oul shite-arse, is it?!

THOMAS.   It is. You observed well.

MAIRTIN.   We'll see about that so, you fecker....

THOMAS.   Oh aye, now. The babby's angry.... *(Mairtin starts clambering up out of the side of the grave to get at Thomas, who takes his truncheon out in readiness. Just as Mairtin gets to his feet, the sound of Mick's shovel splintering the rotten coffin lid under his feet is heard.)*

MICK.   I'm through to it. *(Mairtin and Thomas stare at each other a moment, then forget their fight and go and stand over Mick at the grave. Mick crouches down, so he's almost of out sight, to pull up the rotten boards.)*

THOMAS.   Prepare yourself so, Mick, now. She'll be a shock to you.

MICK.   The boards are ... funny. The boards are already broke open, or is that just the rot, now? *(Mick throws a couple of bits of rotten board away.)*

THOMAS.   Dig some more of that dirt off there, Mick. *(Mick takes his shovel and scrapes some more of the dirt from the coffin. After a few seconds, his scraping starts becoming more frantic.)*

MICK.   What's the...? What's the...?

THOMAS.   Is she...?

MAIRTIN.   This is a peculiar business. *(Mick throws the shovel away and ducks down into the grave again, this time desperately scraping the dirt away with his bare hands.)*

MICK. *(Frantic.)* Where is she...?! Where is she...?!

THOMAS. *(Quietly.)* Is she not...?

MICK. *(Shouting, voice almost breaking.)* She's not there! *(His scraping ceases. Pause. He stands back up, dirty and bedraggled, looking down into the grave numbly. Quietly.)* She's not there. *(Pause. Blackout.)*

SCENE THREE

Night, a day or two later. Set the same as in Scene One. Three skulls and their sets of bones lie on the table in front of Mairtin who stares dumbly down at them, swaying, drunk, blowing bubbles. He has a mallet in one hand and a quarter-empty bottle of poteen in the other, from which he takes disgusted sips every now and then. Mick can be heard rummaging through a toolbox offstage. He is also drunk.

MICK. *(Off.)* There's another one here somewhere I know.

MAIRTIN. What do you be wanting an oul woody hammer for, Mick, now?

MICK. *(Off.)* They do call them mallets.

MAIRTIN. Ohh. *(Pause.)* Skulls do be more scary on your table than they do be in their coffin. Why? I don't know why. Some reason now.

MICK. *(Off.)* Are you getting scared, you wee pup?

MAIRTIN. I'm not getting scared at all. All right I'm getting a bit scared. You won't be leaving me on me own more long?

MICK. *(Off.)* The minute I find this feck I'll be with you. No chance of you helping me look.

MAIRTIN. *(Absently.)* No. *(Pause.)* Weren't they terrible heathens whoever pinched your missus on you?

MICK. *(Off.)* They were. And if I ever got me hands on the fecks, then we'd see.

MAIRTIN.   What would you do to them, Mick? Would you give them a kick?

MICK.   *(Off.)* It would be worse than a kick.

MAIRTIN.   Would you peg stones at them?

MICK.   *(Off.)* Worse than stones it'd be.

MAIRTIN.   Peg ... biteens'a ... rocks....

MICK.   *(Off.)* You wouldn't have heard tell of who took her, Mairtin? Not one of your oul mates, I'm thinking?

MAIRTIN.   None of my mates. What would one of my mates be wanting with your oul missus? My mates don't be fooling with dead missuses.

MICK.   *(Off.)* And can we rule you off the list of suspects too?

MAIRTIN.   I'm on no list of suspects. If I was to be digging up your missus it's good money I'd be wanting for the job, the same as you, cash in hand. Maybe it was a set of tinkers dug her up on you.

MICK.   *(Off.)* What would tinkers be wanting with her?

MAIRTIN.   I don't know. Maybe they were expecting another praitie blight and felt like something to be munching on ahead of time. Not that there'd be much to munch on with your missus. No willy anyways. As far as I know anyways, I didn't know the woman. I still can't believe that about them willies. That's an awful thing.

MICK.   *(Off.)* Found the feck! *(Mick enters, a half-empty bottle of poteen in one hand, a mallet in the other, which he shows to Mairtin.)*

MAIRTIN.   What will be playing so, Mick? That oul game with the hoops and the sticks they do play in England with the hoops and the sticks and the balls they do play in England, what's it called, with the hoops and the sticks? They do play it in England. It has a 'c'.

MICK.   Are you looking in me eyes now, Mairtin?

MAIRTIN.   What eyes?

MICK.   *My* eyes.

MAIRTIN.   Aye, your eyes. *Croquet!*

MICK.   Did you have anything to do with my wife going missing?

MAIRTIN.   Eh?

MICK. Did you have anything to do with my wife going missing?

MAIRTIN. No. *(Mick keeps staring at Mairtin for a long time, as Mairtin sways slightly but returns the stare.)*

MICK. You have looked me in the eyes and I believe you now, Mairtin. I do apologise for even asking you.

MAIRTIN. Good-oh. *(Mick shakes Mairtin by the hand and walks over to the table.)*

MICK. Are these skulls still scaring you?

MAIRTIN. I'm less scared now but don't be leaving me on me own again with them. When they get me on me own they do go smiling at me. Especially that one.

MICK. Shall we be teaching them a lesson then so?

MAIRTIN. Sure you can't teach skulls lessons. They have no brain to be sticking the ... lesson....

MICK. Knowledge?

MAIRTIN. Knowledge. They have no brain to be sticking the lesson through the holes knowledge into.

MICK. This is the only lesson skulls be understanding. *(He brings the mallet crashing down on the skull nearest to him, shattering it, spraying pieces of it all over the room.)* He won't be smiling no more.

MAIRTIN. You've buggered him to skitter!

MICK. I have. Not skitter enough. *(Mick starts smashing the skull into even smaller pieces and stamping on the bits that have fallen on the floor. Mairtin stares at him dumbfounded.)*

MAIRTIN. Ease them in the lake you said.

MICK. In front of the fat one I said, aye. Batter the shite out of them is nearer the mark. And why not? If it's whispering about me they're going to be through the years, what more should they expect when they wind up in my hands than batter?

MAIRTIN. Nothing more.

MICK. Nothing more is right.

MAIRTIN. May I be having a batter, Mick? Ah let me now.

MICK. Why else have I invited you here with a hammer in your hand?

MAIRTIN. I can? Ohh Jeebies.... Good-bye Daniel Faragher. You've been smiling at me long enough, boy. *(Mairtin takes a little run-up and starts smashing another of the skulls and its bones to pieces.*

36

The smashing continues more or less unabated by at least one of the men throughout most of the rest of the scene.)

MICK.   That one's Biddy Curran, not Dan Faragher at all.

MAIRTIN.   Biddy Curran, ya currant bun, ya....

MICK.   She was a fat oul bitch.

MAIRTIN.   She's thin enough now, God bless her. And getting more thin.

MICK.   The middle one's Dan, and Dan's mine. *(Mick starts smashing the middle skull.)*

MAIRTIN.   Ar, you've done two and I've only done one, Mick, ya snatching feck.

MICK.   Don't be going crying, Mairtin. And haven't you had half a bottle of poteen off me today if I'm such a snatching feck?

MAIRTIN.   I have. *(Drinks.)* You're not a snatching feck at all. You're a generous man.

MICK.   You can join in with Dan's bones if you like.

MAIRTIN.   I'll be taking a pop at Biddy Curran's pelvis and then I'll see how I'm feeling.

MICK.   Good-oh.

MAIRTIN.   Should you not be putting a whatyoucall down to be catching them?

MICK.   What matter?

MAIRTIN.   Or a thing?

MICK.   If you'll not be liking my skull-battering ways you can be off with you.

MAIRTIN.   Your ways is fine indeed.

MICK.   I do have a dustpan and brush.

MAIRTIN.   I was thinking. Good-bye Biddy Curran or whatever it is your name is. You're all mixed up now anyways, you poor feck you.

MICK.   Don't be cursing now, Mairtin.

MAIRTIN.   I won't be.

MICK.   Not when you're handling the departed, now.

MAIRTIN.   This is more fun than hamster-cooking!

MICK.   It is. Or if it is I don't know. I've never cooked hamsters.

MAIRTIN.   I've only cooked one hamster. It's not all it's cracked up to be. You stick him in alive and he comes out dead. The feck hardly squeals ... I mean, the fella hardly squeals. If the oven had had a see-through door it would've been more fun, but

37

it didn't, it had an ordinary door. My mistake was not planning ahead. I was egged on. But this is more fun. Is skull-hammering more fun than wife-into-wall-driving, Mick?

MICK.   Oh Mairtin, you're getting a bit near to the mark there, boy.

MAIRTIN.   Oh I am. When I drink I do get awful stupid. I apologise, Mick.

MICK.   I accept your apology, Mairtin. Seeing as you're drunk as Jaysus.

MAIRTIN.   I *am* drunk as Jaysus. But I'll be putting me head in a bucket of water when I get home and I'll be fine then. I do do that of a Saturday night I do, and me dad does never twig I've been drinking.

MICK.   Be remembering to take your head out of the bucket afterwards is the main thing.

MAIRTIN.   I know. Else you'd go drowning.

MICK.   Is right. (*Mairtin stops hammering abruptly, to launch into his story, and Mick stops quickly also, to listen.*)

MAIRTIN.   Did my brother ever tell you the drunk out in Salthill, lay down on the floor to sleep, and where was his head resting? His head was resting in a potty of wee. Drowned he did! On wee! Eh?

MICK.   On wee, was it?

MAIRTIN.   Drowned on wee. What a way to go, eh?

MICK.   Was it his own wee? (*Slight pause.*)

MAIRTIN.   I don't know if it was his own wee or not. And I don't care. He drowned on wee is all I'm saying.

MICK.   No, now. A fact like that is very important, now. Your brother would be the first to agree.

MAIRTIN.   (*Pause.*) Now that I think of it, I think my brother *did* want to launch an investigation into the matter, but they wouldn't let him. But I don't know if it was whose wee it was was what aroused his suspicions or not. Sure, a pig that smelt would arouse that bastard's suspicions. Thinks he's Starsky and Hutch. (*Pause.*) I, for one, would rather drown on me own wee than on anybody else's. Though I'd rather not drown on wee at all!

MICK.   I had three uncles drowned on sick.

MAIRTIN.   (*Pause.*) But, sure, drowned on sick is nothing to go shouting about. Doesn't everybody drown on sick?

MICK.   Three uncles now, I'm saying.

MAIRTIN.   Three uncles or no. Drowned on sick is ten-a-penny now, Mick. A million have drowned on sick. Oul black fella. Jimi Hendrix. Drowned on wee I'm talking about. Drowned on wee you have to go out of your way. Drowned on sick you don't. And of course. Sick is there in your gob already. Wee is nowhere near.

MICK.   If it's drunk you are and you go to bed and you fear you may be sick, this is what you should do.... *(He lays down flat on his belly on the floor, his face to one side.)* Lay down flat on your belly or on your side, your face turned to the side of the pillow. Or throw the pillow away completely would be the best thing.

MAIRTIN.   I don't need advice from you, Mick Dowd, on not drowning on sick. I know well.

MICK.   Like this, now.

MAIRTIN.   I know like that, and your floor is filthy.

MICK.   This is what I always remember on going to bed, no matter how much of a sup I've had, this is what I always remember *(Almost tearfully.)* in mind of me three poor uncles, were young men.

MAIRTIN.   Get up anyways, now, because it wasn't sick was the subject at all. You do always be changing the subject on me. Wee was the subject.

MICK.   *(Getting up.)* Three uncles, I'm saying.

MAIRTIN.   I know, three uncles.

MICK.   And one of them in America.

MAIRTIN.   In America? I suppose people do drown on their sick in America too. Oh of course.

MICK.   In Boston Massachusetts.

MAIRTIN.   In Boston Massachusetts?

MICK.   In Boston Massachusetts. He did drown on his sick.

MAIRTIN.   I suppose at least he'd travelled. *(Pause.)* Good-oh. *(The two almost simultaneously begin smashing up the bones again.)*

MICK.   We should have music as we're doing this.

MAIRTIN.   *(Blankly.)* Music, music....

MICK.   Music to hammer dead fellas to. I have a Dana record somewhere....

MAIRTIN.   Put Dana on so. *(Mick puts on a record of "All Kinds of Everything"* by Dana.)*

*See Special Note on Songs and Recordings on copyright page.

39

MICK. I didn't think young people liked Dana nowadays.

MAIRTIN. They may not but I do. I've liked Dana since I was a child. If I met Dana I'd give her a kiss.

MICK. She wouldn't be kissing you, ya get.

MAIRTIN. For why? *(Mairtin stops hammering, looking sad and serious. Mick stops and looks at him.)*

MICK. Why wouldn't Dana be kissing you?

MAIRTIN. Aye.

MICK. *(Pause.)* Well maybe she would, now.

MAIRTIN. On the lips.

MICK. *(Shrugging.)* Maybe she would.

MAIRTIN. Although she's born-again Christian now.

MICK. Honestly, Mairtin, I'd avoid her. *(Mick starts hammering again, and after a few seconds Mairtin joins him.)*

MAIRTIN. *(Pause.)* Would you be hammering your missus's bones with equal fervour were she here, Mick?

MICK. I wouldn't be. I'd have some respect.

MAIRTIN. Maybe a favour it was they did you so, the fellas went and stole her on you?

MICK. No favour was it to me, and if I had the feckers here, then you'd be seeing some fancy skull-battering. I'll tell you that. Battered to dust they would be!

MAIRTIN. Good enough for them, the morbid oul fecks. And not only stealing your missus then, if that weren't enough, but to go pinching the locket that lay round her neck too, a locket that wouldn't fetch you a pound in the Galway pawn, I'd bet. *(Mick has stopped hammering on the locket's first mention and stepped back a pace, staring at Mairtin whose hammering continues unabated, entirely unaware of his faux-pas.)*

MICK. The rose locket, was it?

MAIRTIN. The rose locket, aye, with the picture of you. What use would the fecks have in taking that, other than just to taunt you? *(Mick sits down in the armchair, the mallet in his lap, still staring at Mairtin, who continues ahead with the skulls.)* The miserable heathen gets, and that's all they are. It was probably the same ones stole me *Star Wars* men on me when I was four, when I left them out in the rain. It was Han and Luke and … was it Chewie? No, I didn't have Chewie. It was Han and Luke and some other one

40

they had off me ... Princess Leia! Aye, and them are the three best ones in *Star Wars*. You can't play *Star Wars* without them. Look at you sitting there! Be getting back to work you, ya slack feck you, or I'll have a word with oul Welsh Welsh to be docking your wages on you. Welsh.

MICK. In a minute now, Mairtin. I've to sit down and be having a think a minute.

MAIRTIN. *(Stopping hammering.)* That's what all the clever kids at school do do is sit down and be having a think, when it's out in the yard playing football they should be, and getting some sun on their arms. You can't budge the freckle-faced fecks, not even with a dig. *(Pause.)* Ah good luck to them, they're not harming anyone. Why should I be ordering them about and giving them digs? They've every right to be sitting. *(Pause.)* I do get in an awful happy mood when it's out of me brains I am, Mick.

MICK. I can see.

MAIRTIN. I could kiss fools and feck dogs. *(Pause.)* Have we done enough hammering for the meantime so?

MICK. We have.

MAIRTIN. What's next on the agenda?

MICK. Be picking up a few of the big lumps, there, and be putting them in the sack. *(Mairtin does so, drunkenly.)*

MAIRTIN. Ah there's too many of the bastards to be picking up. You should get a hoover.

MICK. Just a few more of the big ones will do us.

MAIRTIN. I was promised a dustpan and brush a while back. I see that promise proved untrue. Now what?

MICK. *(Standing.)* Now we'll be driving them out to the lake to be starting the disposing.

MAIRTIN. With a string of prayers said over them, Mick?

MICK. With a string of prayers said over them. I'll be getting me car out now, unless I don't suppose you'd want to be driving, Mairtin?

MAIRTIN. Ah you wouldn't let me be driving, would ya?

MICK. If you're not up to the job, no I wouldn't be.

MAIRTIN. I'd be up to the job, Mick! I'd be up to the job!

MICK. You're not a tadeen over the limit, now?

MAIRTIN.   I'm not near the limit, sure. I've had a bare sip. Oh let me be driving, Mick. Please now. *(Pause. Mick takes his car keys out of his pocket and tosses them to Mairtin, who fumbles them at length and drops them, then drunkenly picks them back up off the floor.)* Oh jeebies, this has turned into a great oul night. Driving and drinking and skull-battering.... *(Mairtin dashes out through the front door, leaving his sack behind him.)*
MICK.   Be bringing your bag of skulleens now, Mairtin! *(Pause. Mairtin returns slowly, smiling, and picks up the sack.)*
MAIRTIN.   I'd forget me head if it wasn't screwed up. *On.* Me mam does say 'You'd forget your head you would, Mairtin.' I say oh aye. *(He exits with the sack. Off.)* I'll be sure and remember to be putting me seat-belt on too, Mick, knowing your track record. *(Sound of Mairtin laughing, off.)*
MICK.   *(Quietly.)* Be doing what you like, ya feck.... *(He picks up his mallet and rolls it around in his hand a little.)* It'll make no difference in the end. *(He exits briskly, bringing the mallet with him and turning the lights off behind him, as the sound of a car starting up is heard.)*

SCENE FOUR

Mick enters, turns lights on. His shirt is covered in blood. He wipes some blood off his mallet and lays it on the table, then brushes the bone fragments littering the floor into the next room. He sits in his armchair when finished. There is a knock at the door. Mick let's Maryjohnny in.

MARY.   Mick.
MICK.   Maryjohnny.
MARY.   Cold.
MICK.   I suppose it's cold.
MARY.   Oh, now, it's cold, Mick.
MICK.   Well, it's *night* I suppose.

MARY.   Oh it's night, aye.

MICK.   I suppose a sup would you be after?

MARY.   Ah only if you're having one, Mick, now. *(Mick pours them two glasses.)* I've just come from the bingo.

MICK.   Oh aye, and how many times tonight did you win?

MARY.   Only three times tonight, Mick. One of me fluorescent pens ran out on me.

MICK.   Uh-huh, that's always the worry with fluorescent pens. You had a bad night of it so.

MARY.   Two free goes on the bumpy slides at the Leisureland swimming is all they gave me. I won't get much use out of them. *(Pause.)* You wouldn't want them, Mick?

MICK.   I wouldn't, Mary. I was never a man for bumpy slides. Never saw the sense in them.

MARY.   I'll give them to Mairtin or someone so. Is Mairtin able to swim? *(Mick wipes some of the blood from himself.)*

MICK.   I'd bet money against it.

MARY.   What's all that on you, Mick? Out painting have you been?

MICK.   I have, aye. I've been out painting red things.

MARY.   That'll stain.

MICK.   Ah it's just an oul work-shirt, Maryjohnny. What harm?

MARY.   No harm. *(Pause.)* I heard tell of your Oona going missing on you, Mick. That was a terrible thing. If you can't be let rest when it's seven years dead you are, when can you be let rest?

MICK.   You can never be let rest.

MARY.   I couldn't bear to think of anyone running off with my bones when I'm dead.

MICK.   No one'll run off with your bones, Maryjohnny. Sure, they'd need a small truck to begin with.

MARY.   A small truck for why?

MICK.   No why. Just a biteen big-boned sometimes you do seem.

MARY.   I'm not big-boned. I'm just a bit fat is all.

MICK.   A bit fat, oh aye, aye. A bit fat indeed.

MARY.   It's a peculiar mood tonight you're in, Mick.

MICK.   It is. It must be them paint fumes or something.

MARY. *(Pause.)* Did you hear Ray Dooley's lost his tour guide job?

MICK. I did. Sure, if you go pegging shite at Americans you're bound to lose your tour guide job.

MARY. You are.

MICK. And cracking Vietnam jokes then.

MARY. Off to Boston for his brother's wedding next month he is.

MICK. Next month, is it? That wasn't a very long engagement. Me and Oona five years we were engaged, and it was five years we well needed. To get to know each other's faults and the like, y'know, and to accept them then.

MARY. What was Oona's biggest fault, Mick?

MICK. Oona didn't have big faults really. She just had little faults. Niggly things, y'know? She'd never wrap up cheese properly. Y'know, when she was finished with it. She'd just leave it lying about, letting the air get to it. The same with bread. She'd never wrap up bread properly. Y'know, like after she'd made a sandwich or the like. And she was terrible at scrambled eggs, and I don't know why, because scrambled eggs are easy to do. Oona's scrambled eggs'd come out either grey or burned.

MARY. You don't miss her so.

MICK. I *do* miss her. I mean, that scrambled egg business wasn't really a big thing. We'd just avoid having scrambled eggs, y'know? *(Pause.)* I miss the talk of her. Oona could fill the house with talk. And she'd always stand up for me against people. Y'know, in a fight or something, or if people were saying things agin me. She'd've been the first to defend me if she heard the town was saying I murdered her on purpose.

MARY. It's a shame she's dead so. *(Pause.)* I wonder who it was took her?

MICK. Uh-huh? *(Thomas knocks and enters, carrying a small bag.)*

MARY. Evening, Thomas. Cold.

THOMAS. What are you doing up here?

MARY. I was passing on me way from the bingo.

THOMAS. I thought I told Father Welsh to bar you from the bingo.

44

MARY.   You did but Father Welsh reinstated me to the bingo.

THOMAS.   So he countermanded official police orders, did he? I'll have to be looking into that one. You run along home now, Gran. I want to speak to Mick alone.

MARY.   I've only just got here, sure.

THOMAS.   I don't care if you've only just got here. That's an official police order, I'm saying.

MARY.   Don't you go official police ordering me, Thomas Hanlon, the number of times I wiped the dribbling skitter off the bare babby's backside of ya.

THOMAS.   *Please* Gran.

MARY.   I'll go when I've finished me sup and not before.

MICK.   What would you want to be speaking to me alone for anyways?

THOMAS.   Oh nothing terrible important really. Just I'd like you to write out and sign a little oul confession for me, that's all. Just a weeny little confession, like.

MICK.   A confession to what? *(Thomas takes a skull with a large forehead-crack out of his bag.)*

THOMAS.   A confession to the murdering be blunt instrument, or be some sort of instrument, of your late wife, Mrs. Oona Margaret Dowd. *(Thomas gestures to the skull crack.)*

MARY.   No...!

MICK.   Oh. Okay so.

THOMAS.   Hah?

MICK.   Okay, I said. Do ya have a pen?

THOMAS.   *(Checks himself.)* I don't. Don't you have one? *(Mick looks for a pen.)*

MICK.   I have one somewhere, I know.

MARY.   *(Takes out bingo pens.)* I have me bingo pens. They're flourescent but they don't all work.

THOMAS.   Sure fluorescent pens are no good for filling out confessions, sure!

MARY.   A yalla one?

THOMAS.   No. 'A yalla one', Jesus.

MICK.   *(Finding pen.)* Here, me lucky lotto pen. Now, what exactly do you want me to be saying, Thomas?

THOMAS. Well, the *truth*, Mick.

MICK. Oh, the truth, aye. Fair enough. *(Mick writes out his confession on two pieces of paper Thomas gives him, as Mary picks the skull up.)*

MARY. It's true? *(Pause.)* I had always prayed only fool gossiping is all it ever was. If I had known that....

MICK. If you had known that you'd still've come up cadging booze off me all these years, ya cheapskate fecking lump.

THOMAS. Don't you go calling my granny a cheapskate fecking lump, ya murdering oul ghoul, ya.

MICK. Murdering oul what ya?

THOMAS. Ghoul, ghoul.

MICK. Oh, ghoul. I thought you said 'whore'.

THOMAS. And don't go criticising me pronunciation either!

MICK. *(To Mary.)* You just put my wife's skull down now you, you and your flourescent fecking pens. Look at as many flourescent pens she has, Thomas, when bingo's supposed to be a bit of fun and a bit of fun to raise a few bob for them poor oul fecks in Africa. Out the mouths of starving darkies Maryjohnny rips her bingo winnings, but I see you don't go getting her confessing.

MARY. Isn't it better to starve darkies than to murder missuses?

MICK. Not at all is it better, and put my Oona down now, you, I've told you once. I don't want the pooh-stench of your manky hands grubbing all over her. *(Mary puts skull down and continues drinking. Mick writes.)* Where was it you found her, Thomas?

THOMAS. Down the bottom of our fields I found her.

MICK. The bottom of yere fields, oh aye. Down beside the bones of that dead cow Mairtin was telling us about the other day, I'll bet. The one he said wandered in and fell down dead, when doesn't the world and his wife know he dragged that cow screaming from Pato Dooley's place and hit it with a brick, and it's only as easy-going as Pato is he never pressed charges.

THOMAS. That's only circumstantial evidence.

MICK. No, that's only *hearsay* evidence.

THOMAS. Feck I'm always getting them two beggars mixed up. What harm? It isn't knowing the difference between hearsay and circumstantial evidence that makes you a great copper. No. Detective work it is, and going hunting down clues, and never letting a case drop no matter what the odds stacked against you, no matter how many years old.

MARY.   Like *Petrocelli.*

THOMAS.   Like *Petrocelli* is right, Gran, and the first thing I do when they promote me is reopen the case of that lettuce and jam man I was telling you about, 'cos I can't sleep nights sometimes thinking of that poor fella's murder going four years unsolved, as cold and alone in his big fat grave he lies.

MICK.   And the fella who drowned on wee is another.

THOMAS.   And the fella who drowned on wee is another. I may bring a urine expert in on that one.

MICK.   What's another word for 'convulse'? I've used 'convulse' once and I don't want to be repeating meself.

THOMAS.   *(Thinking.)* Convulse, convulse, convulse.... *Spasm.*

MICK.   Spasm, spasm, spasm.... Good one. *(Writes.)*

THOMAS.   I have a great vocabulary me, I do, oh aye. *(Pause.)* Are you nearly done?

MICK.   I'm nearly done, all right.

MARY.   Poor Oona. Why did you kill her, Mick? Sure, bad scrambled eggs is no just cause to butcher your wife.

MICK.   I know it's not, Mary, and do you want to hear something funny? I *didn't* butcher my wife. Just like for seven long years I've been saying I didn't butcher my wife. I never butchered anybody 'til tonight. *(He gives his confession to Thomas, who reads through it at speed.)* A pure drink-driving was all my Oona was, as all along I've said, but if it's a murderer ye've always wanted living in yere midst, ye can fecking have one.

THOMAS.   D'you think I'm going to believe this pile of fecking bull? Down the disco with Ray Dooley tonight Mairtin is, and nowhere but the disco.

MICK.   But, sure, if down the disco Mairtin was, how would I have ended up with his bastard brains dripping down the bloody front of me?

MARY.   No...!

MICK.   D'you see how great a copper he is, Maryjohnny, with his skulls and his solving and his lettuces in empty fridges, yet

47

doesn't bat an eye at a blood-soaked man standing whap-bang in front of the feck-brained fool....

THOMAS. You killed him?

MICK. I did, aye. His body's hanging halfway out the wind screen of me Anglia a mile away there. *(Thomas dives for Mick, knocking him off his chair and strangling him on the floor, Mick barely defending himself.)*

MARY. Leave him, Thomas, leave him! Thomas! *(Mairtin enters behind her, somewhat concussed, a big bloody crack down the centre of his forehead, dripping onto his shirt. He watches the fight a while, Mary noticing him after a few seconds, confused.)*

MAIRTIN. What are them two gobshites up to? *(Thomas stops strangling Mick. Both stand and stare at Mairtin.)* What are ye's feckers looking at? Ye's *fellas* looking at, I mean? *(Thomas examines Mairtin's wound. Mary sits, refilling drink.)*

MARY. How are you, Mairtin?

MAIRTIN. I'm fine, Gran, although a biteen of a headache I do have, aye. What are you doing pawing at me, you? *(Thomas rubs Mairtin's face gently.)*

THOMAS. We have you now, Michael Dowd. We have you now. *(Thomas takes his handcuffs out and goes to Mick.)*

MAIRTIN. Have him for what?

THOMAS. Have him for ramming a mallet through the poor brains of you.

MAIRTIN. A mallet? What are you talking about, sure? A pure drink-driving is all this was.

THOMAS. Hah?

MICK. Hah?

MAIRTIN. A pure drink-driving is all this was. What would Mick want to go malleting my poor brains for? Mick likes me an awful lot, don't you, Mick?

MICK. I do, Mairtin. Sure I think you're a great fella.

MAIRTIN. See, Thomas? Mick thinks I'm a great fella. *(Behind Thomas's back, Mick picks up the confession and sets it alight. It slowly burns as Thomas questions Mairtin.)*

THOMAS. Listen, Mairtin, concussed is all you are now, and who wouldn't be....

MAIRTIN. I'm not all concussed. It'd take more than a major car-crash to concuss me, I'll tell ya.

THOMAS. But didn't he just sign a confession saying he hacked through the drunken skull of ya?

MAIRTIN. Did ya, Mick?

MICK. No, no, I didn't, Mairtin.

MAIRTIN. There you go.

THOMAS. What d'you mean you didn't? Don't I have the fecking thing right here...? *(Thomas turns to see the last corner of the confession burning to ash.)*

MICK. You've cocked it up again, haven't ya?

THOMAS. Mairtin? Listen to me. You're going to come down to the station with me, now, and you're going to swear out how Mick it was tried to kill you tonight....

MAIRTIN. Oh Jesus, can't you just leave poor Mick alone and in peace, you, *McMillan and Wife?*

THOMAS. Don't keep calling me *McMillan and Wife*, I've told you twenty fecking times!

MAIRTIN. If he said he didn't kill his missus that's good enough for me, and let it rest.

THOMAS. What are you on his fecking side for?!

MAIRTIN. Well why wouldn't I be on his fecking side, when it's me own blackguard brother I catch carving a hole in Mick's missus's skull there, the day after you'd dug her up on him.

THOMAS. Shut up about that digging...!

MAIRTIN. I won't shut up about that digging and I'll tell you why I won't shut up about that digging! Because not even a fecking pound would the Galway pawn give me for that rose locket, and you said it'd get me at least ten. *(He gives Mick the locket.)* Only gave me that to shut me up, he did, Mick, but I realise that'd be nothing more than stealing from ya, and not only stealing from ya but stealing from the poor dead wife of ya, and anyways the fella in the pawn said it was just a piece of shite not worth pissing on, so it's no great loss, ya know what I mean, like?

THOMAS. Are you finished, Mairtin?

MAIRTIN. *(Pause. Confused.)* Am I Finnish?

THOMAS. Are you *finished*, I said.

MAIRTIN. Oh, am I finished? *(Thinks awhile.)* No I'm not finished, Mr. high-and-mighty detective bollocks. Heh, detective me arse, when the whole of Leenane knows you'd have trouble arresting a shop-lifting child, if the child confessed with the chocolate round his gob. Or if you did arrest him you'd arrest him for killing the Kennedys.

THOMAS.   Is that right?

MAIRTIN.   It is. Sure it's only 'cos you're so good at helping kids across the road that you're even tolerated in this job.

THOMAS.   You're finished now, are ya?

MAIRTIN.   I'm finished for the minute, aye, but I may be thinking up some more insults for ya in a whileen once I get me breath back.

THOMAS.   But for the time being you're finished?

MAIRTIN.   For the time being I'm finished, aye. Sure haven't I just said five times.

THOMAS.   Good-oh *(Thomas smashes Mairtin twice across the head with the mallet, Mairtin collapsing to the floor.)*

MARY.   Thomas! *(Mick forcibly restrains Thomas from hitting Mairtin any more.)*

MICK.   Leave him, Thomas, Christ! Thomas!

MAIRTIN.   *(Dazed.)* What did he do that fer? *(Thomas stares at Mick blankly a while, sucking a second on his inhaler, Mick still holding him by the arms.)*

THOMAS.   I think ... I think ... I think they're never going to promote me. *(Mick lets Thomas go. Mairtin has crawled onto a chair. In a blank daze, Thomas caresses Mairtin's cheek, then gently touches his bloody head.)*

MAIRTIN.   *(Quietly, worried.)* Are you all right there, Tom? *(Thomas nods blankly.)*

THOMAS.   I'll get you for all this someday, Mick Dowd. On me own soul I swear it.

MICK.   Good luck so. *(Thomas nods, glances at the skull and at Mick, then exits. Mick sits with his wife's skull in his hands. Mary dabs at Mairtin's bloody head with a hanky, Mairtin yelping slighting in pain.)*

MAIRTIN.   Ar Gran, ya bitch! *(Mary tuts.)* Ar Gran ya eejit, I meant. There'd better be none of your mouldy oul snot on that hanky now, Gran.

MARY.   There's not, Mairtin. This is just me hanky for show.

MAIRTIN.   Your hanky for show? Uh-huh? *(He gives Mick a look as if Mary is mad.)* D'ya hear this one?

MICK.   I think maybe to hospital you should be going for yourself, now, Mairtin. A bang on the head can be awful serious if not looked at.

MAIRTIN.   Ar hospitals are for poofs, sure.

MICK.   Hospitals aren't for poofs. They let anybody in.

MAIRTIN.   For poofs and for lesbos who can't take a middling dig. *(Mary tuts.)* Wha? 'Lesbos' isn't swearing.

MARY.   Is it not?

MAIRTIN.   No. It's short for lesbians, y'know.

MARY.   Oh.

MAIRTIN.   'Lesbos'. Y'know, like Mona McGhee in me school with the beard. *(Pause.)* Five times I've asked that bitch out and she still won't go.

MICK.   There's nothing the matter with lesbians, Mairtin. They're doing no harm to anybody.

MAIRTIN.   They're not, I suppose. And they're great at tennis. Em, you can leave me now, Gran. You're sort of getting on me nerves now, so you are. *(Mary stops attending to Mairtin and watches Mick with skull a while.)* I suppose that'd be your missus, would it, Mick?

MICK.   It would.

MAIRTIN.   Uh-huh. Has she changed much since last you saw her.

MICK.   *(Pause.)* She has, Mairtin.

MAIRTIN.   Oh aye, it's been seven years, I suppose.

MARY.   *(Pause.)* Do you like bumpy slides, Mairtin?

MAIRTIN.   Bumpy slides? Where the hell did bumpy bloody slides come from?

MARY.   I won two goes on the bumpy slides at Leisureland if you'd want to go.

MAIRTIN.   You won't catch me going on the bumpy slides with you, missus. I'd look a pure fool.

MARY.   No, you could bring somebody else, I'm saying. *(She gives Mairtin the tickets.)*

MAIRTIN.   Oh. Aye. Thank you, Gran. Maybe Mona'd want to go. Heh, this has been a great oul day, this has. Drinking and driving and bumpy slides, and that oul battering them skulls to skitter was the best part of the whole day. *(Mary stares at Mick sternly.)* Would you need any help in giving your Oona a batter, Mick, or will you be handling that one yourself, now?

MICK.   I'll be handling this one meself, Mairtin.

MAIRTIN.   Good-oh.

MICK.   And I'll be sending you a bill for the damage to me Anglia before the week's out.

MAIRTIN.   Ar that's not fair, Mick.

MICK.   Well life's not fair, Mairtin.

MAIRTIN.   *(Confused slightly.)* It *is* fair. I like it anyways. *(He gets to his feet and is overcome with dizziness. He sways around the room on weak legs and only manages not to collapse by clinging onto a wall.)* Em, I think I might pop into that hospital after all. A biteen dizzy I am. I'll be seeing ye.

MICK.   Be seeing you, Mairtin.

MAIRTIN.   *(Pause.)* Be seeing you, Gran, I said!

MARY.   Be seeing you, Mairtin.

MAIRTIN.   Jeez, *deaf. (Mairtin takes a deep breath then staggers across the room, swaying, just making it out through the door, which he pulls behind him.)*

MARY.   So you do hammer the bones to skitter so.

MICK.   Tonight was the first time ever that hammering happened, Maryjohnny, and only because wasn't I pure upset at Oona going missing on me....

MARY.   And you expect me to believe you, the lies you never stop spouting?

MICK.   What lies?

MARY.   A fool could see Mairtin's injuries were no accident.

MICK.   And, sure, didn't I admit that one outright, and sign a confession to the fact? How was that a lie?

MARY.   And the lies o'er your poor Oona's dying then.

MICK.   Oh you're still not going on about that fecking one, are ya? I have never lied o'er Oona dying. Never once.

MARY.   Oh no? I must've been mistaken what I saw that night so, as along the two of ye drove.

MICK.   What did you see? There was nothing to see.

MARY.   Oh I suppose there was nothing to see, now.

MICK.   If you've something to say to me, go ahead and say it outright and stop beating around the bush like a petrified fecking lummox. If you had seen anything made you think I'd killed Oona deliberate, why so would you've still come visiting me every night for the past seven year? *(Mary finishes off her poteen with a flourish and puts the glass down.)* Oh, just to cadge me fecking booze, was it? Well be off on the road for yourself if that's the only reason you come here, with your hour-long weather bulletins and your Eammon fecking Andrews spouting then. I never laid a finger on Oona, not from the day we married to the day she died, and if it's that you think you can upset me saying you saw something that night when there was nothing to see, then you've got another fecking think coming, girlie.

MARY. I'm saying nothing. Nothing at all am I saying. All I'm saying is you'll be meeting up with Oona again someday, Mick Dowd, and not just the bare skull but the spirit of her, and when you meet may down to the stinking fires of Hell she drag the rotten murdering bones of you, and may downhill from there for you it go. Good-bye to you now. *(Mary moves to the door.)*

MICK. Maryjohnny? *(Mary turns.)* You've forgotten your fluorescent pens, there. *(She picks the pens up.)*

MARY. Thank you. *(Mary goes to the door again.)*

MICK. And Maryjohnny? *(Pause.)* I didn't touch her. I swear it. *(Mary stares at him a moment, then exits. Mick looks at the rose locket then picks up the skull and stares at it awhile, feeling the forehead crack. He rubs the skull against his cheek. Quietly.)* I swear it. *(He caresses the skull again, then kisses the cranium gently. Lights slowly fade to black.)*

PROPERTY LIST

Poteen (MICK)
2 drinking glasses (MICK)
Cigarettes (MAIRTIN, THOMAS)
Lighters or matches (MAIRTIN, THOMAS, MICK)
Shovels (MAIRTIN, MICK)
Bits of wood (MICK)
Large, dirty black cloth sack, with bones and skulls (MAIRTIN)
Skull with lock of hair (MICK)
Asthma inhaler (THOMAS)
Mallets (MAIRTIN, MICK)
Bottle of poteen, three-quarters full (MAIRTIN)
Bottle of poteen, half full (MICK)
Music record (MICK)
Car keys (MICK)
Fluorescent pens (MARY)
Small bag with skull with large forehead crack in it (THOMAS)
Pen (MICK)
2 pieces of paper (THOMAS)
Handcuffs (THOMAS)
Hanky (MARY)

SOUND EFFECTS

Car starting

NEW PLAYS

★ **HONOUR by Joanna Murray-Smith.** In a series of intense confrontations, a wife, husband, lover and daughter negotiate the forces of passion, history, responsibility and honour. "HONOUR makes for surprisingly interesting viewing. Tight, crackling dialogue (usually played out in punchy verbal duels) captures characters unable to deal with emotions ... Murray-Smith effectively places her characters in situations that strip away pretense." *–Variety* "... the play's virtues are strong: a distinctive theatrical voice, passionate concerns ... HONOUR might just capture a few honors of its own." *–Time Out Magazine* [1M, 3W] ISBN: 0-8222-1683-3

★ **MR. PETERS' CONNECTIONS by Arthur Miller.** Mr. Miller describes the protagonist as existing in a dream-like state when the mind is "freed to roam from real memories to conjectures, from trivialities to tragic insights, from terror of death to glorying in one's being alive." With this memory play, the Tony Award and Pulitzer Prize-winner reaffirms his stature as the world's foremost dramatist. "... a cross between Joycean stream-of-consciousness and Strindberg's dream plays, sweetened with a dose of William Saroyan's philosophical whimsy ... CONNECTIONS is most intriguing ..." *–The NY Times* [5M, 3W] ISBN: 0-8222-1687-6

★ **THE WAITING ROOM by Lisa Loomer.** Three women from different centuries meet in a doctor's waiting room in this dark comedy about the timeless quest for beauty – and its cost. "... THE WAITING ROOM ... is a bold, risky melange of conflicting elements that is ... terrifically moving ... There's no resisting the fierce emotional pull of the play." *–The NY Times* "... one of the high points of this year's Off-Broadway season ... THE WAITING ROOM is well worth a visit." *–Back Stage* [7M, 4W, flexible casting] ISBN: 0-8222-1594-2

★ **THE OLD SETTLER by John Henry Redwood.** A sweet-natured comedy about two church-going sisters in 1943 Harlem and the handsome young man who rents a room in their apartment. "For all of its decent sentiments, THE OLD SETTLER avoids sentimentality. It has the authenticity and lack of pretense of an Early American sampler." *–The NY Times* "We've had some fine plays Off-Broadway this season, and this is one of the best." *–The NY Post* [1M, 3W] ISBN: 0-8-222-1642-6

★ **LAST TRAIN TO NIBROC by Arlene Hutton.** In 1940 two young strangers share a seat on a train bound east only to find their paths will cross again. "All aboard. LAST TRAIN TO NIBROC is a sweetly told little chamber romance." *–Show Business* "... [a] gently charming little play, reminiscent of Thornton Wilder in its look at rustic Americans who are to be treasured for their simplicity and directness ..." *–Associated Press* "The old formula of boy wins girls, boy loses girl, boy wins girl still works ... [a] well-made play that perfectly captures a slice of small-town-life-gone-by." *–Back Stage* [1M, 1W] ISBN: 0-8222-1753-8

★ **OVER THE RIVER AND THROUGH THE WOODS by Joe DiPietro.** Nick sees both sets of his grandparents every Sunday for dinner. This is routine until he has to tell them that he's been offered a dream job in Seattle. The news doesn't sit so well. "A hilarious family comedy that is even funnier than his long running musical revue *I Love You, You're Perfect, Now Change*." *–Back Stage* "Loaded with laughs every step of the way." *–Star-Ledger* [3M, 3W] ISBN: 0-8222-1712-0

★ **SIDE MAN by Warren Leight.** 1999 Tony Award winner. This is the story of a broken family and the decline of jazz as popular entertainment. "... a tender, deeply personal memory play about the turmoil in the family of a jazz musician as his career crumbles at the dawn of the age of rock-and-roll ..." *–The NY Times* "[SIDE MAN] is an elegy for two things – a lost world and a lost love. When the two notes sound together in harmony, it is moving and graceful ..." *–The NY Daily News* "An atmospheric memory play ... with crisp dialogue and clearly drawn characters ... reflects the passing of an era with persuasive insight ... The joy and despair of the musicians is skillfully illustrated." *–Variety* [5M, 3W] ISBN: 0-8222-1721-X

DRAMATISTS PLAY SERVICE, INC.
440 Park Avenue South, New York, NY 10016 212-683-8960 Fax 212-213-1539
postmaster@dramatists.com   www.dramatists.com

NEW PLAYS

★ **CLOSER by Patrick Marber.** Winner of the 1998 Olivier Award for Best Play and the 1999 New York Drama Critics Circle Award for Best Foreign Play. Four lives intertwine over the course of four and a half years in this densely plotted, stinging look at modern love and betrayal. "CLOSER is a sad, savvy, often funny play that casts a steely, unblinking gaze at the world of relationships and lets you come to your own conclusions ... CLOSER does not merely hold your attention; it burrows into you." *—New York Magazine* "A powerful, darkly funny play about the cosmic collision between the sun of love and the comet of desire." *—Newsweek Magazine* [2M, 2W] ISBN: 0-8222-1722-8

★ **THE MOST FABULOUS STORY EVER TOLD by Paul Rudnick.** A stage manager, headset and prompt book at hand, brings the house lights to half, then dark, and cues the creation of the world. Throughout the play, she's in control of everything. In other words, she's either God, or she thinks she is. "Line by line, Mr. Rudnick may be the funniest writer for the stage in the United States today ... One-liners, epigrams, withering put-downs and flashing repartee: These are the candles that Mr. Rudnick lights instead of cursing the darkness ... a testament to the virtues of laughing ... and in laughter, there is something like the memory of Eden." *—The NY Times* "Funny it is ... consistently, rapaciously, deliriously ... easily the funniest play in town." *—Variety* [4M, 5W] ISBN: 0-8222-1720-1

★ **A DOLL'S HOUSE by Henrik Ibsen, adapted by Frank McGuinness.** Winner of the 1997 Tony Award for Best Revival. "New, raw, gut-twisting and gripping. Easily the hottest drama this season." *—USA Today* "Bold, brilliant and alive." *—The Wall Street Journal* "A thunderclap of an evening that takes your breath away." *—Time Magazine* [4M, 4W, 2 boys] ISBN: 0-8222-1636-1

★ **THE HERBAL BED by Peter Whelan.** The play is based on actual events which occurred in Stratford-upon-Avon in the summer of 1613, when William Shakespeare's elder daughter was publicly accused of having a sexual liaison with a married neighbor and family friend. "In his probing new play, THE HERBAL BED ... Peter Whelan muses about a sidelong event in the life of Shakespeare's family and creates a finely textured tapestry of love and lies in the early 17th-century Stratford." *—The NY Times* "It is a first rate drama with interesting moral issues of truth and expediency." *—The NY Post* [5M, 3W] ISBN: 0-8222-1675-2

★ **SNAKEBIT by David Marshall Grant.** A study of modern friendship when put to the test. "... a rather smart and absorbing evening of water-cooler theater, the intimate sort of Off-Broadway experience that has you picking apart the recognizable characters long after the curtain calls." *— The NY Times* "Off-Broadway keeps on presenting us with compelling reasons for going to the theater. The latest is SNAKEBIT, David Marshall Grant's smart new comic drama about being thirtysomething and losing one's way in life." *—The NY Daily News* [3M, 1W] ISBN: 0-8222-1724-4

★ **A QUESTION OF MERCY by David Rabe.** The Obie Award-winning playwright probes the sensitive and controversial issue of doctor-assisted suicide in the age of AIDS in this poignant drama. "There are many devastating ironies in Mr. Rabe's beautifully considered, piercingly clear-eyed work ..." *—The NY Times* "With unsettling candor and disturbing insight, the play arouses pity and understanding of a troubling subject ... Rabe's provocative talc is an affirmation of dignity that rings clear and true." *—Variety* [6M, 1W] ISBN: 0-8222-1643-4

★ **DIMLY PERCEIVED THREATS TO THE SYSTEM by Jon Klein.** Reality and fantasy overlap with hilarious results as this unforgettable family attempts to survive the nineties. "Here's a play whose point about fractured families goes to the heart, mind – and ears." *—The Washington Post* "... an end-of-the millennium comedy about a family on the verge of a nervous breakdown ... Trenchant and hilarious ..." *—The Baltimore Sun* [2M, 4W] ISBN: 0-8222-1677-9

DRAMATISTS PLAY SERVICE, INC.
440 Park Avenue South, New York, NY 10016 212-683-8960 Fax 212-213-1539
postmaster@dramatists.com   www.dramatists.com

NEW PLAYS

★ **AS BEES IN HONEY DROWN by Douglas Carter Beane.** Winner of the John Gassner Playwriting Award. A hot young novelist finds the subject of his new screenplay in a New York socialite who leads him into the world of *Auntie Mame* and *Breakfast at Tiffany's*, before she takes him for a ride. "A delicious soufflé of a satire … [an] extremely entertaining fable for an age that always chooses image over substance." —*The NY Times* "… A witty assessment of one of the most active and relentless industries in a consumer society … the creation of 'hot' young things, which the media have learned to mass produce with efficiency and zeal." —*The NY Daily News* [3M, 3W, flexible casting] ISBN: 0-8222-1651-5

★ **STUPID KIDS by John C. Russell.** In rapid, highly stylized scenes, the story follows four high-school students as they make their way from first through eighth period and beyond, struggling with the fears, frustrations, and longings peculiar to youth. "In STUPID KIDS … playwright John C. Russell gets the opera of adolescence to a T … The stylized teenspeak of STUPID KIDS … suggests that Mr. Russell may have hidden a tape recorder under a desk in study hall somewhere and then scoured the tapes for good quotations … it is the kids' insular, ceaselessly churning world, a pre-adult world of Doritos and libidos, that the playwright seeks to lay bare." —*The NY Times* "STUPID KIDS [is] a sharp-edged … whoosh of teen angst and conformity anguish. It is also very funny." —*NY Newsday* [2M, 2W] ISBN: 0-8222-1698-1

★ **COLLECTED STORIES by Donald Margulies.** From Obie Award-winner Donald Margulies comes a provocative analysis of a student-teacher relationship that turns sour when the protégé becomes a rival. "With his fine ear for detail, Margulies creates an authentic, insular world, and he gives equal weight to the opposing viewpoints of two formidable characters." —*The LA Times* "This is probably Margulies' best play to date …" —*The NY Post* "… always fluid and lively, the play is thick with ideas, like a stock-pot of good stew." —*The Village Voice* [2W] ISBN: 0-8222-1640-X

★ **FREEDOMLAND by Amy Freed.** An overdue showdown between a son and his father sets off fireworks that illuminate the neurosis, rage and anxiety of one family – and of America at the turn of the millennium. "FREEDOMLAND's more obvious links are to *Buried Child* and *Bosoms and Neglect*. Freed, like Guare, is an inspired wordsmith with a gift for surreal touches in situations grounded in familiar and real territory." —*Curtain Up* [3M, 4W] ISBN: 0-8222-1719-8

★ **STOP KISS by Diana Son.** A poignant and funny play about the ways, both sudden and slow, that lives can change irrevocably. "There's so much that is vital and exciting about STOP KISS … you want to embrace this young author and cheer her onto other works … the writing on display here is funny and credible … you also will be charmed by its heartfelt characters and up-to-the-minute humor." —*The NY Daily News* "… irresistibly exciting … a sweet, sad, and enchantingly sincere play." —*The NY Times* [3M, 3W] ISBN: 0-8222-1731-7

★ **THREE DAYS OF RAIN by Richard Greenberg.** The sins of fathers and mothers make for a bittersweet elegy in this poignant and revealing drama. "… a work so perfectly judged it heralds the arrival of a major playwright … Greenberg is extraordinary." —*The NY Daily News* "Greenberg's play is filled with graceful passages that are by turns melancholy, harrowing, and often, quite funny." —*Variety* [2M, 1W] ISBN: 0-8222-1676-0

★ **THE WEIR by Conor McPherson.** In a bar in rural Ireland, the local men swap spooky stories in an attempt to impress a young woman from Dublin who recently moved into a nearby "haunted" house. However, the tables are soon turned when she spins a yarn of her own. "You shed all sense of time at this beautiful and devious new play." —*The NY Times* "Sheer theatrical magic. I have rarely been so convinced that I have just seen a modern classic. Tremendous." —*The London Daily Telegraph* [4M, 1W] ISBN: 0-8222-1706-6

DRAMATISTS PLAY SERVICE, INC.
440 Park Avenue South, New York, NY 10016 212-683-8960 Fax 212-213-1539
postmaster@dramatists.com www.dramatists.com